Recognising Workforce Health as a Key Organisational Asset: A Study of Current Thinking and Practice

by

Robin Roslender
Howard Kahn

Heriot-Watt University

Joanna Stevenson
Formerly of University of Stirling

Published by

The Institute of Chartered Accountants of Scotland
CA House, 21 Haymarket Yards
Edinburgh EH12 5BH

First Published 2009
The Institute of Chartered Accountants of Scotland

© 2009
ISBN 978-1 904574-56-9
EAN 9781904574569

This book is published for the Research Committee of
The Institute of Chartered Accountants of Scotland.
The views expressed in this report are those of the authors
and do not necessarily represent the views of
the Council of the Institute or the Research Committee.

No responsibility for loss occasioned to any person acting
or refraining from action as a result of any material
in this publication can be accepted by the authors or publisher.

Printed and bound in Great Britain
by T. J. International Ltd.

C ONTENTS

F OREWORD

Everyone would recognise that a healthy workforce can only be good for business, but is a healthy workforce an 'asset' and can or how should it be 'valued' or 'accounted' for as intellectual capital or any other way? This report, which relates closely to prior and forthcoming studies into intellectual capital funded by SATER, compares and contrasts the views of finance directors and human resource directors on this issue, as well as investigating three large organisations which are implementing measures to improve and monitor workforce health.

The most recent *Absence Management Annual Survey Report 2009* by the Chartered Institute of Personnel and Development states that an average of 7.4 days per year per employee is lost to sickness in the UK, with an estimated cost of £692 per employee per year. With a growing interest in corporate social responsibility (CSR) organisations are increasingly looking at incorporating within their CSR policies an emphasis on maintaining a healthy and happy workforce. With such an increased interest in this matter, it is important to consider whether and how workforce health can be accounted for. In this report a wider definition of accounting is considered, looking at both measurement and reporting and not necessarily restricted to the financial statements.

The study identifies that the cost of ill heath can be more easily identified and measured than placing a value for a 'healthy workforce'. Human resource directors are more positive in general regarding the importance of workforce health and the ability to value it, maybe reflecting the fact that finance directors are more aware of the inherent difficulties of valuing intellectual assets. Finance directors prefer the use of narratives and non-financial numbers.

Case studies in three very different organisations (AstraZeneca, South Lanarkshire Council and South West Water) identify activities undertaken to improve and monitor workforce health. This research highlights that the success of such initiatives is dependent upon securing the continuing buy-in at all levels of management.

The report challenges the UK accountancy profession to consider a number of steps, recognising them as very expensive, which might be taken to enable all stakeholders to benefit from a healthier workforce; a concerted effort to promote interest in the intellectual capital field; making practitioners aware of how it may be possible to account for various components of intellectual capital, in particular those surrounding health and wellbeing; to do this in conjunction with other managerial professions, including human resource management and occupational health specialists; and finally by influencing central government to install a portfolio of legislation, compelling employers to take a greater level of responsibility for the health of their workforces.

I look forward to seeing how these challenges may be taken up.

This project was funded by the Scottish Accountancy Trust for Education and Research (SATER). The Research Committee of The Institute of Chartered Accountants of Scotland (ICAS) has also been happy to support this project. The Committee recognises that the views expressed do not necessarily represent those of ICAS itself, but hopes that the project will add to the knowledge and debate about how to improve and account for workforce health.

David Spence
Convener, Research Committee
November 2009

A CKNOWLEDGEMENTS

The successful completion of any research project is greatly reliant on the cooperation of a range of people. Initially the authors wish to thank those individuals who were prepared to complete and return the questionnaires that provide the principal empirical content of this research monograph. Many thanks also to the individuals who made time in their busy work schedules to participate in the interviews at the three case organisations.

The contribution to the production of the draft and final manuscripts made by our colleagues at Heriot-Watt University, Karen Morton, Gemma Blackledge and Kenneth Weir, is similarly appreciated, as is the support offered for our endeavours by colleagues in the Departments of Accountancy and Finance and Management at Heriot-Watt University, and in the Department of Accountancy and Finance at the University of Stirling. Several colleagues in the former Uppsala seminar group on Work Health and Management Control provided many useful insights on the project in its initial stages, particularly Professors Ulf Johanson and Guy Ahonen.

Throughout the duration of the research project we have received continued, good-natured support from Professor Christine Helliar, the former Director of Research at The Institute of Chartered Accountants of Scotland, and her team, Michelle Crickett and Angie Wilkie. As ever, the comments furnished by The Institute's anonymous reviewers have contributed much to the production of an improved research monograph.

In the increasingly demanding arena of 21st century academic research it is those closest to us who invariably find themselves volunteered as our greatest sources of support. Without their tolerance and understanding, expressed in countless ways, we could not achieve very much at all. Many, many thanks, as always.

Finally, the Research Committee and the researchers are grateful for the financial support of The Scottish Accountancy Trust for Education and Research, without which the research would not have been possible.

EXECUTIVE SUMMARY

The observation that 'employees are our most valuable asset' provides the starting point for this study. For those employers who subscribe to it, the implication is that the majority of the existing workforce will be retained, wherever possible. Beyond this, where the opportunity exists to enhance the health, among other attributes, of employees, these employees will as a result become even more valuable assets. When absent from work due to illness, workers cannot contribute to the value creation and delivery process. The fundamental objective of this study, therefore, is to identify the extent to which senior managers in the accounting and finance and human resource management functions in UK organisations currently think of the health and wellbeing of their workforces as a valuable asset.

The study is a contribution to the growing body of literature in the intellectual capital field in which the importance of intellectual capital in the value creation and delivery process continues to be hotly debated. Among the many contributions to this debate, those attributable to the accounting discipline continue to attract considerable attention. Given the accountancy profession's claimed role within the business enterprise, and beyond, it is incumbent upon its leading thinkers to identify how it might be possible to meaningfully account for intellectual capital, alongside the stocks of physical and financial capital. If they are not able to do so, and with some impact on practice, the continuing credibility of the profession and its claimed jurisdiction may be undermined to some extent.

Accounting has two complementary meanings: measurement and reporting. For many practitioners, the measurement of intellectual capital equates with placing a financial value on it, reflecting the paradigm that has served the profession well in the case of both physical and financial capital. The difficulty, however, is that many constituents of intellectual capital are characterised by their subjectivity. In addition, many have also not been purchased by the business and thus lack any historical cost. For this reason a significant part of the accounting for intellectual capital literature has focused on the development of non-financial metrics that are able to capture the 'growth' of stocks of intellectual capital within the business enterprise.

Having abandoned the attempt to derive objective, financial valuations, it follows that there is no necessity to restrict the reporting of intellectual capital growth to the traditional financial statements. Consequently, alongside many engaging contributions on the formulation of relevant intellectual capital metrics, the intellectual capital accounting literature has encompassed a range of attempts to identify possible reporting frameworks. Of these the most familiar have been the Swedish Skandia Navigator and Intangible Assets Monitor frameworks, both of which date back to the mid 1990s, together with the Balanced Scorecard, which dates back a little earlier. More adventurous reporting approaches have subsequently evolved, again with Scandinavia in the vanguard, in which reporting combines both measurement and narrative elements.

Among the many constituents of intellectual capital, those associated with 'people', or human capital, are especially problematic to account for. An extensive literature dating back to the early 1960s documents the efforts of accounting academics to 'put people on the balance sheet'. By and large this research failed to produce a satisfactory outcome, so much so that as the intellectual capital concept entered the broader management literature, 'accounting for people' had become of limited interest to accounting researchers. The challenge thrown down by the need to account for intellectual capital has had the effect of reviving interest in accounting for people, which is again a thriving site for enquiry.

To date the UK has not been one of the leading sites for intellectual capital accounting research in general, or accounting for people in particular. This was the case even at the height of interest in human resource accounting in the 1970s. For whatever reason, such challenges do not seem to excite or enthral UK accounting academics nor their practitioner counterparts. In recent years, however, The Institute of Chartered Accountants of Scotland has actively supported a number of researchers interested in intellectual capital or intangibles, as one facet of their promotion of the business reporting concept. The other UK professional associations have followed suit to some extent but overall it would be wrong to claim that these are 'hot topics' as they are in Scandinavia, Australia, the Far East and in southern Europe.

Against this backcloth the following pages report the findings of a study of current UK thinking and practice regarding workforce health viewed as a key constituent of human capital and, thereby, a potential source of competitive advantage. Questionnaires were mailed to the accounting and finance directors and HR directors of 1,000 UK organisations, drawn from both the private sector and public sector. Recipients were questioned about how their organisations currently view issues surrounding the health and wellbeing of their workforces, their understanding of the intellectual capital phenomenon and how the two might merge around the over-arching theme of 'workforce health as an organisational asset'. The dominant emphasis is on the accounting perspective, with both accounting and finance and HR directors being questioned on how it might be possible to account for workforce health. A further set of insights is derived from interviews with representatives of three organisations that might be considered to be in the vanguard of UK thinking and practice in relation to the promotion of greater levels of workforce health and wellbeing.

The survey responses indicate that human resource (HR) directors believe that both physical and mental health issues are viewed favourably within their organisations to a rather greater extent than their counterparts in the accounting and finance function. The same pattern is evident in terms of their respective views on the extent of monitoring of health and wellbeing, its measurement and reporting and the prospects for future development of health and wellbeing provision. Only in the case of the existence of steps currently being taken to promote improved health are the responses from the two samples more in accord with each other. Overall, those accounting and finance directors employed in private sector organisations returned the least encouraging responses, a pattern repeated throughout the findings.

The accounting and finance directors claim greater familiarity with the terms 'intellectual capital' or 'intangibles' than their human resource counterparts. Although when questioned about their knowledge of how to account for intellectual capital, neither sample are very familiar, with the Balanced Scorecard being the most widely recognised approach. The HR directors are generally more positive about the benefits of attempting to account for intellectual capital, with almost a third of accounting and finance directors believing such exercises are a distraction. Given the consensus across the management literature regarding intellectual capital's contribution to value creation and delivery, this is a cause for some concern within the UK.

The HR directors are also more disposed to viewing workforce health as an organisational asset, with over two thirds believing that it is possible to identify some form of financial value for this purpose. Accounting and finance directors, however, are less convinced of the possibility of such valuations, recognising the merits of using non-financial numbers, narratives or some combination of these, which could also incorporate alternative financial numbers. When questioned about reporting on workforce health to external stakeholders, as opposed to simply accounting for it, accounting and finance directors are more attracted to the use of supplementary information, either stand alone narratives or narratives in combination with financial data. HR directors, possibly less aware of the detail of the debates that surround this issue, prefer a combination of financial information and narratives incorporated within the financial statements.

Access to three organisations was used to garner more detailed insights on the issues associated with viewing workforce health as an organisational asset. All three readily agreed to the use of their names in this report. The global pharmaceuticals company AstraZeneca and its predecessors (ICI, Zeneca and Astra) have been engaged in workforce health and wellbeing promotion since the mid 1970s, while South Lanarkshire Council's involvement dates back to the beginning of this decade; South West Water's involvement lies between them. In all three cases it is evident that a critical factor in successfully promoting higher levels of workforce health and wellbeing is to secure the continuing buy-in at all levels of management for ensuring that the organisation's workforce health strategy is implemented, affirmed and monitored. It is also evident that mental health issues have now overtaken those associated with physical health, with the result that more emphasis is being placed upon maintaining health and wellbeing rather than simply seeking to restore it. The growing incidence of mental health problems, and the time taken to recover from many of them, could result in ill health becoming more expensive, with all parties only at the beginning of the process of identifying which interventions are most likely to prove successful.

In the light of the modest interest in, and indeed concern for, workforce health and wellbeing evident among the present sample of accounting and finance directors, the study concludes by identifying a number of steps the UK accountancy profession might take to address this state of affairs. Initially, the professional accounting institutes need to incorporate further discussion of the intellectual capital topic within their examination syllabi, thereby highlighting its relevance for the 21st century accounting practitioner. The continuing importance of promoting increased levels of workforce health and wellbeing within organisations must also be emphasised in tandem with providing encouragement to engage with the challenges entailed in measuring and reporting on it to a range of stakeholders. Such interventions are more likely to be successful if they are pursued in association with other management specialists, with whom the profession should also work in concert to lobby government for the funding necessary to provide improvements to health infrastructure.

1 INTRODUCTION

Background

During the last thirty years, health and accounting have become increasingly interrelated in the UK and other advanced societies. As a consequence of the continued advance in medical science, it has become possible to keep a growing proportion of the population alive and in relatively good health. The cost of doing so, however, has increased significantly with the result that it has become accepted that sound financial management is necessary if society is not to be swamped by the cost of providing the levels of healthcare now technically possible. Although health, as the determinant of life, is arguably the most precious human attribute, others such as education, safety, national security and social inclusion are similarly expensive to provide, thereby increasing the pressure to ensure 'best value' in the delivery of high levels of national health. Put simply, the role of accounting in relation to this challenge is to implement the same regime of cost management in the provision of healthcare as is desirable in the provision of more traditional goods and services. The only difference in the case of publicly funded health care provision, as in the UK, is that rather than seeking to make a greater profit, the objective is to derive more benefit from the finite financial resources that are available for this purpose.

This study brings together health and accounting on a very different basis. Rather than viewing health as a cost to be managed, it views health as an asset that is to be valued, although not necessarily literally. In the following pages the focus is on workforce health rather than health in general. While the two are intimately linked, workforce health necessarily resides with those who are in employment and relates to those manifestations of health, and more specifically ill health, which are causally linked to being in employment. Work has always been recognised to cause a whole range of illnesses, which in turn lead to absence, diminished capacity to contribute in the workplace and, for many, early retirement or even death. It still remains an open question whether workforce ill health is a greater or a lesser problem in the 21st century, although current patterns of sickness absence suggest the former.

If workers are absent from work through illness, they cannot contribute to the value creation and delivery process. If levels of sickness can be reduced, their capacity to do so is enhanced. At the limit, if there was no workforce ill health, value creation and delivery capacity would be at the maximum. This being so, it is very easy to understand why this study seeks to represent workforce health as an asset. In doing so, it follows in a long tradition of accounting thinkers who have designated workers as human assets or human resources. Both human assets and workforce health should be valued, although not in the usual sense of placing a financial valuation on them, thereby allowing their incorporation within financial statements in some way. Here the term 'valued' means that employees and their health are accorded the importance that they merit given their contribution to the value creation and delivery process. In the case of employees this already occurs via the mechanism of differential rewards, which refers to the issue of cost, since wages and salaries are invariably represented within financial statements as costs.

Accounting for intellectual capital

Like the term 'cost', 'asset' has strong accounting associations. The accountancy profession has long been engaged in the task of accounting for assets, fixed and current, tangible and intangible, principally by determining their value and thereby providing a means of incorporating them within financial statements, especially the balance sheet, alongside 'liabilities', 'capital' and 'retained profit'. Many members of the accountancy profession would immediately recognise workforce health as an intangible asset, and in all likelihood a very intangible asset, and consequently like human assets, very difficult to account for in an objective way.

Since the mid 1990s there has been a growing interest in accounting for a wide variety of such assets as employee expertise, company reputation, knowledge networks or workforce health, now referred to as 'intangibles' or alternatively, as in this study, 'intellectual capital'. While not all in the intellectual capital field would agree that there is little likelihood of identifying robust financial valuations for such assets, thereby allowing them to be included within financial statements, the broad consensus is that softer quantitative information, narrative accounts or some combination of these offers the most appropriate means to account for intellectual capital. At this time Scandinavian thinking on accounting for intellectual capital continues to be the most advanced, followed by contributions from Australia, the Far East and southern Europe, with North America seemingly committed to more traditional accounting approaches. Interest in the UK has been limited, despite The Institute of Chartered Accountants of Scotland's continuing willingness to provide funding for this and several related studies in recent years.

Consequently, in the course of enquiring about the extent to which senior managers in UK organisations view workforce health as a valuable asset, it seems apposite to also probe their current understanding of the intellectual capital phenomenon together with how it might be possible to begin to account for workforce health as an example of such value creating assets.

Structure of the report

Chapters two and three provide literature reviews on intellectual capital and workforce health respectively. The former begins with a brief discussion of the new wealth of nations before outlining what the intellectual capital concept incorporates. This is followed by a discussion of some of the main issues involved in accounting for intellectual capital and in the relatively limited attention that such issues have attracted to date in the UK. Chapter three begins by outlining what the study identifies as workforce health. Attention then turns to the present extent of the sick leave problem in the UK as evidenced in employee absence from work. The case for identifying workforce health as a further element of intellectual capital is then made, followed by a discussion of how it might be possible to account for employee health. Drawing on the two previous chapters, the fourth chapter initially sets out the research questions that inform the study. This is followed by a discussion of the research design the research team has adopted, details about how the samples used in the two surveys were constructed and how the questionnaires were administered. Chapters five and six report the findings of two surveys of accounting and finance directors and HR directors, while the seventh chapter reports some of the insights gained from three case studies in which leading-edge thinking and practices were evident. The concluding chapter eight summarises the main findings of the study and discusses the implications for the UK accountancy profession.

2 The Intellectual Capital Phenomenon

Introduction

This chapter provides an introduction to the intellectual capital phenomenon by means of a brief review of the growing body of literature about it. After outlining a number of significant societal changes relevant to understanding intellectual capital, its principal components: human capital; relational capital; and structural capital, are discussed. The focus then switches to attempts to account for intellectual capital that have been pursued during the past decade and their links with the longer established challenge of accounting for the human factor. The hitherto limited interest in the intellectual capital phenomenon in the UK context is considered. The chapter concludes with a brief summary of its main points.

The new wealth of organisations

In the mid 1990s a number of writers began to talk about intellectual capital as constituting an increasingly important basis for value creation (Brooking, 1996; Edvinsson and Malone, 1997; Stewart, 1997; Sveiby, 1997). This was particularly so in the context of knowledge organisations, which were becoming more evident as advanced societies began to evolve into mature post-industrial forms. Within the emergent knowledge economy, intellectual capital was touted as providing the new wealth of organisations. It was therefore necessary to manage the organisation's stocks of intellectual capital effectively to ensure continuing success within the global marketplace. This in turn provided further impetus to develop knowledge management, already a fashionable topic

(Nonaka and Takeuci, 1995; Bartlett and Ghoshal, 1997; Davenport and Prusak, 1997), in a more holistic way, replacing its founding technical emphases with a more people-centred cultural perspective (Mouritsen and Larsen, 2005).

The use of the term intellectual capital conveys a continuity in thinking with the traditional foundations of value creation in organisations. In previous eras capital was first identified with the buildings and machinery (physical capital) that were combined with labour in order to produce the mass of manufactured goods that characterised the industrial society. Subsequently it became recognised that monetary resources (financial capital) played an increasingly important role in mature manufacturing economies, in which huge capital investments were necessary to ensure continued participation within the marketplace, now rapidly extending worldwide. The recognition that intellectual forms of capital were becoming critical to the latter process marked an acknowledgement that over time labour, as the source of most of this form of capital, was no longer to be viewed as a resource to be combined with industrial or financial capital. It was now to be recognised as providing the foundation upon which these more traditional forms of capital might be put to best use.

The realisation that knowledge, and those who might be designated knowledge workers, are becoming more important within contemporary society is not just a recent phenomenon. During the 1960s commentators were becoming interested in an interrelated set of changes that were observable in the most advanced societies, soon to be designated the post-industrial society (Galbraith, 1967; Touraine, 1971; Bell, 1974). One of the key changes was the emergence of new occupational categories including government employment, the service industries, the leisure sector, financial services and education. In order to meet these new occupational needs, greater numbers of young people experienced higher education, giving rise to a more enlightened populace. The creation, consolidation and communication of ideas and knowledge was becoming an increasingly important social phenomenon. Many of these advances might be available not only to the most advanced societies but also to the rest of human kind in a world that was already beginning to become more finite. In general there was great optimism about the emergence of a new social order, reflecting the spirit of the age and its 'baby boom' younger generation.

Twenty years later, the knowledge society and the intellectual capital phenomenon had assumed a much more hard-edged significance. Successful knowledge companies were now being accorded market values far in excess of their accounting-based book values. An obvious explanation was that the intellectual capital of these enterprises was responsible for such discrepancies, since many of its constituents could not be assigned values within the prevailing accounting and reporting framework. At the extreme, in leading edge hi-tech companies, the unaccounted for element of market value dwarfed the traditional assets. The subsequent rise of the dot.com enterprises, which invariably had very few traditional assets, saw this discrepancy rise to near astronomical proportions, although by the end of the century, and following some spectacular dot.com crashes, the situation became less extreme. Nevertheless, concerns about the continued impact of the intellectual capital phenomenon on the global capital markets meant that accounting for its 'hidden' value was now something of a priority for the accounting and finance profession.

Definition of intellectual capital

At its simplest, intellectual capital equates with any discrepancy that might exist between the market value of a company and the accounting-based book value that can be derived within the prevailing accounting and reporting framework. The accountancy profession has long been familiar with such discrepancies in the guise of intangible assets, the most common of which is goodwill. When one business acquires another, it is commonplace for the acquiring company to pay more than might be merited if valuation is based solely on book values. Because the acquiring company sees something that it values in the acquisition, it may be willing to pay for it identifying the excess outlay as goodwill to be included in its own financial statements thereafter and accounted for in a prescribed manner. The constituents of goodwill have been widely explored by practitioners and academics alike, in an attempt to better understand how to account for them. This has informed advances in accounting for such intangible assets as brands, know-how, patents, trademarks and customer databases.

Most, if not all, of the commonly identified intangible assets are invariably also listed as examples of intellectual capital, giving rise to the belief that the two terms are largely synonymous. This is further confused by the use of a third term, 'intangibles', when talking about intellectual capital. While it must be acknowledged that intellectual capital refers to a category of value creating assets, it should not be viewed as being identical with the intangible assets designation. At its simplest, all intangible assets are examples of intellectual capital but the latter designation (or alternatively intangibles) extends to types of asset that are intangible but cannot readily be accounted for within the prevailing calculus of valuation that underpins conventional financial accounting and reporting. Although the accountancy profession has been reasonably successful in accounting for, say, brands or customer databases, little advance has been evident in the case of accounting for the human factor, often the critical constituent of any goodwill outlay (Roslender *et al.*, 2007). This observation neatly provides a link with literature contributions that have sought to identify the principal forms of intellectual capital.

A useful starting point is found in the work of Edvinsson, one of the earliest writers on intellectual capital who in the early 1990s was the Director of Intellectual Capital at Skandia AFS, a Swedish financial services company. Edvinsson (1997) distinguishes between two types of intellectual capital: human capital and structural capital. The former encompasses all the capital that belongs to an organisation's employees and includes their skills, experience, expertise, commitment, ingenuity and team working capacity; the attributes that earlier generations have referred to as human assets or human resources. While such assets have always been associated with employees, until recently they have not been regarded as being important to their employers who now realise that it is vitally important to retain people within the organisation as far as possible if continued value creation is to be achieved. Structural capital is described by Edvinsson as being what remains in the organisation when the employees go home for the night: 'dimensions beyond human capital left behind when the staff went home' (p368). By means of the Skandia Value Scheme, he decomposed structural capital into a number of constituents, some of which had long been recognised but a number of which were of a more contemporary nature. As might be imagined, some of the most critical elements of organisational capital are extremely intangible.

Despite its relative novelty as a concept, for much of the past decade there has been a surprisingly high degree of agreement about the tripartite taxonomy of intellectual capital components identified in Brooking (1996) and adapted by Lynn (1998). First, human capital can be composed of many of the attributes identified by Edvinsson and his predecessors in the human asset and human resource accounting tradition. Second, relational capital is the capital that has been created around the process of delivering value to customers outside an organisation. As well as familiar intangible assets such as brands, customer lists and customer databases, relational capital extends to intangible elements such as company reputation, customer loyalty, customer relationships and product recognition, as well as contemporary phenomenon such as efficient supply chains, beneficial business associations and inter-company networks. Third, structural capital is principally made up of a further set of elements within the organisation. Lynn's classification distinguishes between assets such as patents, copyrights, design rights and trademarks, collectively termed intellectual property, that overlap extensively with the intangible assets concept, and infrastructure capital. The latter refers to highly intangible attributes such as corporate culture, management philosophy, knowledge bases, knowledge networks and teams, without which many organisations would not be able to function effectively, and would not be distinguishable from competitors in their particular marketplaces. A number of variants on this generic classification exist, however, including those of Meer-Kooistra and Zijlstra (2001) and Habersam and Piber (2003).

Roslender and Fincham (2001, 2004a) employ a simple distinction between primary intellectual capital and secondary intellectual capital. Primary intellectual capital is identifiable as human capital, encompassing the many attributes that employees bring to the organisation. It is identified as primary on the grounds that human capital is the source of all value in the value creation process. The designation also extends to all employees, reflecting the fact that many in managerial positions are subject to close supervision within modern organisations. Secondary intellectual capital is the totality of knowledge-based assets that have been created by human capital. The more intangible relational capital assets such as company reputation, brand associations, customer loyalty and customer relationships, are the result of human creativity, while more tangible examples such as supply chains or customer databases are outwith this designation despite also being the result of human creativity. Equally, corporate cultures, management philosophies and knowledge networks are examples of secondary intellectual capital, being distinct from information systems or organisation structures. The former differ from the secondary relational capital assets, however, in that corporate cultures, management philosophies and knowledge networks exist to sustain primary intellectual capital, enabling it to better create and deliver value for customers. These ideas are discussed further in the following chapter.

Accounting for intellectual capital

The argument that intellectual capital is the difference between the market and book values of companies poses a very obvious challenge to the accountancy profession, as to how might it be possible to account for intellectual capital. The simplest approach would involve identifying a robust valuation methodology that would permit the determination of a financial value to be incorporated within the financial statements. Such an approach continues attempts at accounting for the various categories of intangible assets, which constitute a subset of intellectual capital.

In the early 1960s Hermanson adopted this approach when he commended human asset accounting to a profession whose efforts did not encompass accounting for this increasingly valuable business asset (Hermanson, 1963, 1964). Eschewing the significance of the observation that, unlike their other assets, businesses did not own employees, Hermanson believed that it would be possible to identify a valuation methodology that would allow businesses to 'put people on the balance sheet', debating the merits of two such approaches: the unpurchased goodwill method; and the adjusted present value method. During the next decade and a half, a plethora of alternative approaches were commended for accounting for the human factor, now in the guise of human resource accounting, which became one of the most researched topics within accounting. Many of these were documented in the first edition of Flamholtz's seminal 1974 monograph - *Human Resource Accounting* (see also Flamholtz, 1985). Flamholtz himself was more ambivalent about the purpose of human resource accounting, although he offered a specific valuation methodology based on individual conditional values. In his view, human resource accounting had more in common with the traditions of managerial accounting than financial accounting and reporting, arguing that it should focus on providing management with financial information about the use of its human resources (a term later to take on increased significance within the personnel profession). Unfortunately, such was the dominance of financial accounting and reporting in the 1970s, Flamholtz was largely unable to escape from the cost and valuation paradigm that underpinned it (Roslender *et al.*, 2007). Consequently, by the early 1980s, following two decades of enquiry, human resource and human asset accounting lacked any consensus about a valuation methodology.

When intellectual capital began to emerge as a major research topic in the mid 1990s, those who were interested in its accounting aspects were attracted by the challenge of identifying precise valuations for these new bases of value creation. Edvinsson (1997) again provides an instructive point of departure for this exercise, in the form of the Skandia Value Scheme, which provides the basis for a series of incremental valuation exercises. In essence Edvinsson argues that it is possible to determine the value of a business's portfolio of intellectual capital assets against a backcloth of a 'balancing' figure which is the difference between market and book value. As a consequence, the problems that are inherent when seeking to account for intangible assets continue to undermine the exercise. In addition, this approach also runs the risk of undervaluing human capital, at least as long as it is envisaged as the balancing figure within the total intellectual capital valuation. There is a danger that, having assembled a series of intellectual capital valuations, the total still falls short of the total 'balancing' valuation, or alternatively exceeds it! Simplicity inevitably produces its own shortcomings but this has not precluded continuing attempts to determine 'accurate' financial valuations (Andriessen, 2004 provides a review of these).

The utility of employing non-financial numbers in management reporting became apparent as a consequence of the emergence of the new management accounting (Kaplan, 1994, 1995). Perhaps recognising the innate limitations of a simple valuation approach to intellectual capital accounting, Edvinsson (1997) suggested that businesses should identify a set of indicators that captured the success with which management had 'grown' their stocks of intellectual capital during accounting periods.

Some of these indicators, such as staff turnover, customer loyalty, new patents registered, were hardly novel; nor was the idea of identifying relevant critical success factors and key performance indicators. Experimentation with these indicators was encouraged so that businesses could better manage their intellectual capital portfolios. To report this information, Edvinsson commended the use of a scorecard format, citing his own experiences with Skandia AFS during the previous five years (Mouritsen *et al.*, 2001a). Similar in form to the Balanced Scorecard, the Skandia Navigator combined performance indicators from five foci: people; customers; process; renewal and development; and financial, to communicate how management visualised its intellectual capital activities (see also Kaplan and Norton, 1996).

An alternative reporting framework was identified by a second Swedish researcher in the form of the Intangible Assets Monitor (Sveiby, 1997). Three categories of intellectual capital are identified, reflecting the prevailing tripartite division discussed earlier: people; customers; and the organisation. In each case three sets of indicators are required for: growth/renewal; efficiency; and stability, giving rise to a three by three grid. Within this basic structure Sveiby commends the use of a traffic light system for ease of reading. A green cell indicates good performance in this field, while a red cell conveys a problematic performance. A yellow colouration signifies the need for concern with performance being on the borderline of unsatisfactory. In addition, the users of the Intangible Assets Monitor framework, of which the Swedish organisation Celemi is the most widely known, are encouraged to provide a brief narrative discussion to supplement the non-financial performance measures, which in turn might be viewed as complementing more traditional financial performance information. Consequently, the Intangible Assets Monitor offers the means of providing a more comprehensive account than might be made available using either the Balanced Scorecard or Skandia Navigator, or similar scorecard approaches such as the Value

Chain Scoreboard (Lev, 2001) or Eriksson Cockpit framework (Starovic and Marr, 2003).

The practice of using a combination of quantitative and narrative information in accounting and reporting on intellectual capital was taken a step forward as a consequence of a Danish Government sponsored initiative that began in 1998 (DATI, 1999) and resulted in the Intellectual Capital Statement approach (DATI, 2001; Mouritsen *et al.*, 2001b; DMSTI, 2003). The initiative was informed by knowledge management thinking, the result of which was that organisations were encouraged to begin their account of their intellectual capital with a reflective knowledge narrative. This serves as the basis for identifying the key management challenges that the organisation faces in seeking to create and deliver value to its customers. The management challenges in turn inform the specific actions taken by management to accomplish this, while the indicators represent this in a more traditional quantitative manner. Management is encouraged to incorporate additional information in such Intellectual Capital Statements by using illustrations, figures and more radical representations as necessary, thereby enhancing the accessibility of the report. Such approaches have subsequently been employed by many Danish organisations. An alternative approach was also developed as a result of the Meritum Project, although to date it has not been as widely subscribed (Meritum, 2002; Bukh and Johanson, 2004; Guthrie *et al.*, 2007).

Roslender and Fincham (2001, 2004a) have taken the narrative approach to accounting for intellectual capital a step forward, in the form of intellectual capital self-accounts. Motivated by the desire to promote an enabling approach to accounting, they argue that self-accounting by primary intellectual (human) capital should be encouraged, including any employee involvement in the creation of secondary intellectual capital. Such 'stories' might initially be made available via the intranets of businesses and other organisations, encouraging interaction among participants. The publication of a set of representative self-accounts would complement the traditional sources of information constructed and made available by organisations. Fincham and Roslender (2003) commented on the overlap between such ideas and the business reporting concept, a topic which has subsequently faded from view to some degree (ICAEW, 2003).

Intellectual capital in the UK

The intellectual capital phenomenon does not appear to have attracted much attention in the UK. The vast majority of the activity identified in the previous sections originates elsewhere, with a significant proportion occurring in Scandinavia. This was the view that Fincham and Roslender (2003) advanced in the conclusion of their earlier ICAS-funded study. The small number of UK empirical studies identified by Roslender and Fincham has not changed much since that time, with Unerman *et al.* (2007, 2008) welcome additions, with a similar pattern evident in the case of discursive contributions. This is in stark contrast to subsequent developments in Scandinavia, Australia, North America and a number of the Pacific Rim countries, as documented in the pages of dedicated academic publications including the *Journal of Human Resource Costing and Accounting* and the *Journal of Intellectual Capital* (see also Guthrie *et al.*, 2007).

Fincham and Roslender argue that the principal issue in respect of accounting for intellectual capital in the UK is how it might be accomplished in practice. Their study found that managers were aware of the emergence of intellectual capital within their own organisations and beyond, and were similarly conscious of its present and continuing importance to the value creation and delivery processes. However, although there were some signs that individuals were beginning to turn their attention to measuring intellectual capital, this was being pursued largely in an ad hoc way. To the extent that there was any attempt to report on intellectual capital growth, this was normally associated with a recognition of the potential of the Balanced Scorecard, a development that had emerged a decade earlier. Awareness of the reporting frameworks outlined in the previous section was close to zero, despite the fact that all were potentially available to accounting practitioners and their colleagues in the other management functions. Fincham and Roslender concluded that some form of educational process was required if the UK accountancy profession was to get to grips with the intellectual capital phenomenon.

This negative conclusion was soon affirmed in the outcome of the *AccountingforPeople* initiative (Roslender *et al.*, 2004; Roslender and Stevenson, 2007). At the beginning of 2003 the Department for Trade and Industry (DTI) launched a consultation process designed to identify the extent of, and best practice in, accounting for people, with the intention of commending to UK businesses desirable mechanisms for providing relevant information on their human resources. The DTI quickly became aware that only a modest extent of accounting for people was practised in the UK, and being quite varied in approach it was unlikely to satisfactorily inform anything beyond an 'evolutionary' approach to the challenge, later confirmed in the Task Force's Final Report published in November 2003. During the following 15 months the initiative's findings were translated into an increasingly minimalist set of requirements for companies to provide information on their people in their financial statements for accounting periods beginning on or after 1 April 2005, with an enhanced Operating and Financial Review acting as a vehicle. However, following the surprise intervention of the then Chancellor of the Exchequer, the proposals were withdrawn in January 2006. Although in principle people information is still a potential constituent of the Business Review which was subsequently made mandatory for company reports, and beyond this for any future Management Commentary (IASB Exposure Draft, 2009).

Both the initial DTI Consultation Paper and the Final Report convey only a minimal attempt to engage with developments within the intellectual capital field, most of which had occurred prior to 2003. Mention is made of the Balanced Scorecard reporting framework, along with the European Foundation for Quality Management (EFQM), Economic Value Added and the work of the Saratoga Institute but there is no acknowledgement of the Skandia Navigator, Intangible Assets Monitor or the Intellectual Capital Statement models (DTI, 2003). The preferred mechanism for reporting people information was the enhanced Operating and Financial Review, abandoned by the Chancellor in his November 2005 intervention. Roslender and Stevenson (2007) take the view that linking the recommendations of the DTI's AccountingforPeople Task Force with the enhanced Operating and Financial Review was a marriage of convenience. Beyond this they question whether the representatives of the UK accountancy profession on the Task Force were really unaware of what are believed to be useful developments within the intellectual capital field. If so, they exhibited a lack of appreciation of recent developments in this field. A more compelling explanation is that they elected to disregard these same developments in order to preserve the status quo, ensuring that the interests of employees remained a very minor consideration for the accountancy profession.

Finally, on a more positive note, in a review of Fincham and Roslender's ICAS monograph, Holland (2006) asserts that there is growing evidence that UK businesses are actively involved in disclosing relevant intellectual capital information, including on employees, to the capital market. This occurs through channels variously designated 'informal', 'private' and 'alternative', one-to-one meetings between company representatives and key analysts and fund managers.

Summary

The success of a growing number of organisations, and not only those engaged in the pursuit of profit, is increasingly recognised to be dependent on their ability to grow their stocks of intellectual capital. As critical organisational assets, they pose an important challenge to the accountancy profession who have developed a range of approaches designed to take them into account in some way. In the case of human capital, arguably the primary form of intellectual capital, continuity with earlier, largely failed attempts to account for the human factor is evident. Unfortunately, to date there has been only a limited attempt to engage these developments in the UK context.

3 WORKFORCE HEALTH

Introduction

This chapter establishes the case for considering workforce health as a further component of intellectual capital. The following section begins by briefly considering health as a personal attribute before moving on to highlight the growing importance of the health dimension of health and safety at work. The third section provides some background information on the present incidence of ill health among the UK workforce and its changing forms. In the fourth section health is identified as an additional element of human capital, something that is placed at the disposal of employers. Workforce health as intellectual capital is based on the axiom that if employees are an organisation's most valuable assets, then a healthy workforce is of even greater value, being something that employers should strive to retain wherever possible. Some discussion of accounting for employee health follows, which identifies some current developments emerging in Scandinavia. The final section provides a summary of the main points of the chapter.

Health - beyond the personal dimension

Health is normally viewed as a deeply personal matter; as a consequence, ill health invariably causes individuals considerable anxiety. Ill health is often shared by family and close friends who are generally prepared to offer their time and energy to act as carers. Individuals are responsible for their own health, albeit though again often shared with their families. As society's understanding of ill health and how to respond to it increases, the call on society's resources also increases, often disproportionately. In those societies in which the costs of ill health are principally borne by the State, health becomes a major political issue as governments wrestle with the resentment that the extra taxation entails. Where funding healthcare on an individual basis already exists, the problem for governments is how to ensure that the necessary safety nets exist to accommodate those who cannot meet their own basic health costs.

The constantly increasing cost of ill health in advanced societies has resulted in healthcare becoming a combination of the traditional approach of curative medicine and preventive medicine. In its State-funded form, preventive medicine is a relatively recent development, dating back to the 1970s. As its name indicates, preventive medicine is intended to educate individuals about how they might become more responsible for their own health and that of those around them. Preventive medicine has given rise to the now common practice of health promotion initiatives designed to reduce what is regarded as avoidable ill health. Smoking has for many years been one activity that the medical profession has sought to curb in the interests of reducing the incidence of heart disease, lung cancer and high blood pressure. More recently, obesity has also been identified as a major cause of ill health that should, if possible, be addressed. Modern medical science is able to treat, if not cure, many of the consequences of smoking or obesity. Although widespread preventive medicine and health promotion are themselves costly activities, on balance they are deemed to provide considerably greater 'value for money' than interventionist medicine and, therefore, have become more politically expedient.

Being in ill health need not preclude an individual continuing to remain within the workforce. Many individuals subject to long-term medication regimes continue to work as normal, as do those who require medication for shorter periods. Employees who become ill with conditions requiring treatment over the short to medium-term, however, often find that they need to be absent from work for some time in order to recover. In many instances they may not suffer any financial consequences of their ill health as their employers may continue to pay them in full until they are fit to resume work. Others are less fortunate, having to rely on State sickness benefits that are significantly less generous than their earnings, hence the increased availability of expensive health insurance products. In both cases the employer may also have to bear the cost of finding temporary cover for absent employees at a cost that can outstrip any savings in wages paid to these employees. Ill health among employees, whatever its cause, poses a problem to employers that translates into a financial cost that most would claim they could do without.

From the perspective of organisational management, the health of employees has traditionally been largely bound up with the health and safety concept. As a consequence, such employees are envisaged as being in ill health because they have been the unfortunate victims of some sort of industrial accident or because of some unintended failure on the part of management to meet safety legislation. Throughout the twentieth century it has been difficult to imagine employers knowingly and wilfully subjecting their workforces to conditions or situations in which they are likely to suffer some form of ill heath, say as a consequence of a fall or similar industrial injury or becoming poisoned, experiencing hearing loss or developing repetitive strain injury. Not only does the incidence of such forms of ill health result in financial penalties and in some of the more tragic cases, substantial payments to those affected, there are the outlays that result from any resulting disruption to employment, in the short, medium or long-term. Nevertheless, beyond these aspects, the health of employees is not something that employers have been overly concerned with beyond taking notice of the admittedly growing burden of health and safety legislation.

In recent times the decoupling of ill heath and working conditions has become more difficult to defend, particularly in those societies that have evolved into the knowledge society stage of post-industrialism. The proportion of the workforce employed in factories is now significantly less than that employed in what was previously termed intellectual labour. Admittedly some of this work is still low in skill content, as exemplified in the ubiquitous 'call centre', despite it having been transferred from the factory floor to the office space. In general, however, the emergence of the knowledge society, with its accompanying information and communication technologies, has resulted in work becoming mentally much more taxing. At the same time, the adoption of managerial philosophies that emphasise the pursuit of maximum efficiency has resulted in severely reduced workforce numbers who often find that the release from the drudgery of the production line that their forebears so desired has been accompanied by even greater demands on their intellectual capacities. The office may have become a safer place to work, but it is by no means a healthier place to pursue employment if current trends in absence from work are anything to go by.

Employee absence from work

The UK Chartered Institute of Personnel and Development's (CIPD) *Annual Survey of Absence Management 2008* reports that on average 3.5% of the individual's working time is currently being lost, or 8 days per year per employee. This is down from 3.7% (= 8.5 days) in 2007 and from a high of 4.4% (10 days) in 2002. Overall, since 2000, the average number of lost days has been 8.8 per year per employee. These figures translate into an average cost to employers of £666 per annum in 2008, marginally up on the equivalent figure of £659 for 2005. The CIPD estimates that, given a total cost to employers in the region of £11.6 billion in 2003, the cost of absence probably exceeded £12 billion in 2006; in 2008 the figure is probably closer to £13 billion. By way of comparison, Almqvist *et al.*, (2007) estimate that in Sweden, a Scandinavian country acknowledged to have a serious sick leave problem, the 2001 loss was 3.9% of working time, at a cost estimated at €2 (£1.4) million per day. The equivalent UK figure for 2001 was 3.8%. The survey reports that in 2008 the UK manufacturing and production sector as a whole exhibited a lower level of lost days than the average, with the food, drink and tobacco industries having a relatively high level of absence while the electricity, gas and water industries had a low level. Private sector service employments were also lower than average with 7.2 lost days per year per employee overall; hotels and restaurants (4.6 days) and IT services (4.4 days) were the best performing sub sectors, with communications and call centres exhibiting much less favourable levels. The public sector as a whole continues to return higher than average levels of absence, losing on average 9.8 days per year per employee, although this was down from 2005 when 10.3 days were lost. The worst performances within the sector were evident in health (11.7 days), followed by central government (11.0 days). Local government organisations appear to have been relatively successful in reducing absence levels, now at 10.1 days per year per employee. Education is the best performing sub sector (7.8 days). Non-profit organisations also recorded slightly worse than the average days lost, with housing associations losing on average 11.0 days per year per employee, while charity services performed relatively well losing 7.6 days.

Absence would appear to be directly related to the size of the employing organisation, with the average days lost in 2008 in units of less than 100 employees being 6.1 compared with 10.8 days in organisations employing between 1,000 and 1,999 people. Large-sized public sector organisation employees lost on average 12.7 days per year per employee due to sick leave. The same pattern continues when length of absence is considered: of those taking sick leave, the level of absence in excess of four weeks is highest, at 29%, in the case of organisations with more than 2,000 employees. It is also highest in public sector organisations. By contrast, the lowest levels of extended absence were reported in organisations employing between 100 and 249 employees and in the private sector service organisations.

In terms of the reported causes of short-term sickness absence, both manual and non-manual employers ranked minor illnesses such as colds, flu and stomach bugs, as a leading cause. In the case of manual workers this was followed by back pain, stress and recurring medical conditions, such as asthma, angina and allergies. Non-manual employers identified stress second, ahead of back pain and recurring medical conditions. Mental ill health, such as clinical depression and anxiety, was identified by 26.0% of non-manual employers and 23.0% of manual employers. The importance of stress in the public services sector is very apparent, with 72.0% of employers identifying it as a cause of short-term absence among non-manual workers, compared with 57.7% in the case of manual workers.

Turning to the causes of long-term absence, stress is the most commonly identified cause among non-manual workers, followed by acute medical conditions, with mental ill health in third place. Public service employees are the worst sufferers in respect of stress and a close second to non-profit organisations in respect of mental ill health. By comparison it is acute medical conditions such as strokes, heart attacks and cancer that trouble manual workers the most, with stress relegated to fourth place and mental ill health in fifth. Taken together, this snapshot suggests that non-manual workers employed in the public sector, arguably the archetypal post industrial employees, are regularly absent from their employments as a consequence of what might be regarded as modern day maladies. Lest it is objected that private sector non-manual workers are no less typical of the post industrial employee, it is worth recording that the CIPD found that 48.5% of employers identified stress as the cause of short-term absence from work and 62.3% as the cause of long-term absence.

The most important cause of stress at work identified by employers was an increased volume of work, well ahead of management style, relationships at work, organisational change and pressure to meet targets. Almost a third of respondents to the survey indicated that stress-related absence continues to increase, with only 11% taking the opposite view. The rate of increase has slowed a little from 2007 when 40% of respondents reported an increase in stress related absence. Once again the public sector fares particularly badly with 46% of public sector employers intimating that stress-related absence is on the increase. The two main causes are identified as being increased workload and organisational change. In their own defence, 60% of respondents continue to believe that reported stress is caused by employees' lives outside of work, with public service employers marginally more sympathetic to the contribution made by workplace factors and more likely to be taking steps to manage it.

The initial observation, that the levels of absence have recently fallen in the UK, from a high in 2002 of 4.4%, is by no means a reason to believe that this phenomenon has passed its peak. If issues outside the workplace are indeed a major contributory factor, as most of the employers surveyed by the CIPD believe, then significant volatility is always possible. Between 2006 and 2007 there was an increase from 3.5% to 3.7% in average working time lost, as people tried to come to terms with an upward trend in interest rates, particularly mortgage rates, rising levels of personal debt, higher heating and food bills. This reduced in 2008, albeit before the current 'Credit Crunch', the full effects of which may not be recognised for some considerable time perhaps. Compounding this are recent concerns about 'presenteeism', where individuals suffering from ill health continue to go to work, often out of fear of losing their jobs and thus their present standard of living (Nielsen *et al.*, 2007). At the extreme, presenteeism could result in major reductions in the value creation and delivery capacities of organisations, the cost of which is largely born by employers. For the present time at least, it seems reasonable to conclude that, like many other advanced societies, the UK is beset with an expensive sick leave problem that needs to be tackled soon for the benefit of all parties.

Workforce health as intellectual capital

Chapter two highlights that human capital encompasses the many attributes that employees bring to their employment and contribute to the value creation and delivery processes of organisations, in most cases in exchange for financial remuneration. Management is tasked to 'grow' these attributes in the pursuit of enhanced value creation and delivery capacity. The latter activities are likely to be more successful in those organisations where a facilitative or enabling organisational culture has been developed and is continuously reproduced by means of continued effective cooperation between employees and their management colleagues. Roslender and Fincham's primary and secondary intellectual capital distinction arguably captures these facets of the intellectual capital management challenge more insightfully (Roslender and Fincham, 2004a). It does not distinguish between managerial and non-managerial employees for the most part, reinforcing the observation that value creation and delivery is necessarily an inclusive process. More significantly it draws attention to the symbiotic relationship that exists between employees and the organisational cultures in which they create and deliver value.

In this regard the health of employees can be considered a further component of primary intellectual capital. Along with their experience and expertise, capacities for learning, leadership and team work, employees bring their health to their employment. Of necessity they also bring their ill health or, more strictly, their capacity to suffer from ill health. This is not to claim that it is work that causes all forms of ill health as this would be a wholly implausible argument to advance. The observations reported in the previous section constitute an acknowledgement that, to some perhaps increased degree, work practices can seriously compromise the health of individuals, particularly their mental health in the modern era. So in the same way that all employees do not exhibit 'perfect' skills, aptitudes, commitment and ingenuity, they also do not exhibit 'perfect' health. A major challenge to the upper echelons of management, therefore, is to ensure that the culture existing within the organisation is such that it ensures that all employees can enjoy the maximum health as well as the best opportunities to develop and utilise their more traditional individual attributes. This is what the concept of a facilitative or enabling organisational culture means in practice. Where this exists, employees, for the most part, will believe that theirs is a good place to work. Others will be attracted to such employments while existing employees will be highly reluctant to seek alternative employment. If these arrangements translate into high levels of performance then such employments may also offer high levels of remuneration, further reinforcing the desire to remain in post.

The observation, often attributed to Peters and Waterman (1982) that: 'our people are our greatest asset', has meant that over the past 20 years the case for retaining the greater part of an existing workforce has gained increased credence in many organisations. It makes good sense to retain those employees who have demonstrated their contribution and commitment to their employers, particularly where specific attributes are in relatively limited supply. It would seem to follow logically that it is in the interests of all parties to ensure that, as far as possible, a workforce is kept in good health. Consequently, senior management is not only tasked with growing its portfolio of human capital as outlined in the previous chapter. It now has the added responsibility of ensuring that levels of ill health resulting from workplace factors are kept to a minimum. Attention will therefore need to be paid to all those aspects of the organisational culture that impinge on employees' health. Known factors such as volume of work, meeting targets, change programmes, structural reorganisation and relocation, will need to be constantly monitored to ensure that any avoidable negative consequences are minimised. Equally important is the need to ensure that preventive health promotion initiatives are a regular feature of the work place. Obvious examples are those related to healthy eating, stopping smoking, alcohol and substance abuse and increased exercise. More generally there needs to be encouragement for all employees to take greater responsibility for ensuring that they are as fit and healthy as they can be, thus complementing any health improvement initiatives introduced by their employers.

Such considerations may seem some distance removed from more familiar examples of intellectual capital like brands, know how and workforce expertise. Yet the 'healthy organisation' *i.e.* one in which health issues are afforded top priority by all participants, would seem to be as critical a necessity for continuing success in value creation and delivery as the learning organisation or the knowledge organisation, concepts that emerged within the intellectual capital field in the mid 1990s (Senge, 1990; Senge *et al.*, 1994; Easterby-Smith *et al.*, 1999). A workforce that displays high levels of individual health, underpinned by significant health awareness, translates into a healthy lifestyle and promises to be more likely to continue to create and deliver value more successfully than one that exhibits lower levels of health. Equally, an organisation that has the necessary infrastructure in place to reproduce its workforce's health profile will also be more likely to succeed in such activities than one that has opted for a more jejune approach to health issues. Employee health and an embedded health promotion regime are, therefore, as much organisational assets as traditional forms of intangible assets or some of the more 'intangible' intangibles that have previously been identified in the intellectual capital literature. The well rehearsed observation that employees can always remove their health from the healthiest organisations should not obscure the fact that all parties have much to gain from ensuring that these same employees remain with their present employers and continue to contribute their value creation and delivery capabilities.

Accounting for workforce health

The desire to place a financial value on the health of individual employees or on the collective health of a workforce has to be tempered with the observation that the infrastructural aspects of the healthy organisation are impossible to value, although gymnasia or similar tangible health and fitness assets will possess an identifiable financial valuations. Consequently, in common with the majority of intellectual capital assets, accounting for them will probably need to be non-financial in approach. The generic Balanced Scorecard reporting framework initially commends itself for this purpose, particularly if one of the perspectives is designated the people perspective as it was in Maisel's (1992) alternative model or as in the Skandia Navigator and Intangible Assets Monitor. Those charged with assembling the information for inclusion in scoreboards of this type are challenged to identify the most appropriate performance metrics on health issues, both lead and lag indicators, and include these in their revamped reports.

The inherent difficulty with such scoreboard approaches is that, while they increase the range and volume of relevant information that is reported, they can only do so in a limited way. Kaplan and Norton originally talked in terms of 12 - 15 indicators being incorporated within their Balanced Scorecard but subsequently increased this to around two dozen (Kaplan and Norton, 1996), thereafter remaining silent on what for them is clearly not the key issue. Nevertheless, even this amount of information is likely to unsettle many in the accountancy profession, not to mention the users of accounting information, particularly if it is reported in different ways by different organisations. Some accounting academics might use these uncertainties to commend the opportunities afforded by a move to a narrative based approach such as an Intellectual Capital Statement or enhanced Operating and Financial Review, which can readily be adapted to incorporate a relatively detailed discussion of employee and organisational health issues. By so doing, they contribute to the process of encouraging the reporting and user communities to recognise the necessity of exploring the merits of a more comprehensive business reporting paradigm (ICAS, 1999).

Consistent with their contributions to the literature of social accounting since the 1970s, Scandinavian academics have begun to consider how it might be possible to progress accounting for workforce health. Several recent papers have identified 'Health Statements' as a means of reporting details on employee health (Grojer and Ahonen, 2005; Mouritsen and Johanson, 2005; Almqvist *et al.*, 2007; Nielsen *et al.*, 2007). As yet such statements are in their embryonic form but several desirable attributes have been identified. Initially these will be self-contained reports that can be used in combination with existing company reporting statements. They will be based in narrative, in much the same way as is evident in the case of the Intellectual Capital Statement. It will be valuable to include both lag and lead information *i.e.* identifying both past successes (and if appropriate failures) and future (improved) health profile target information. In common with developments within the intellectual capital reporting realm, Health Statements should contain the information that the organisation believes is most relevant to those who are employed within it as well as beyond its boundaries. This is not to prejudge that there is no universally valuable information on health and ill health, the case of basic sick leave statistics being the most obvious. Rather, that organisations should view the Health Statement format, in common with similar intellectual capital reports, as providing the opportunity for organisations to visualise their health performance in a reflexive manner.

For many people accounting for health may be a step too far. As intimated at the beginning of this chapter, health has traditionally been viewed as a deeply personal issue, with the implication that it is not something that should be incorporated within accounting framework. This is particularly the case when the focus, as here, is on health in the workplace, information about which might easily be used to further discipline the workforce (Foucault, 1977; Zuboff, 1988; Cooper, 1992; Townley, 1995). As Martensson (2007) and Holmgren *et al.* (2008) have observed, regardless of the good intentions of those, including themselves, who wish to promote the management control of workforce health, this might not have beneficial consequences. Conversely, however, envisioned as a further contribution to social accounting, where the emphasis is on accountability to society, and particularly when combined with the enabling underpinnings associated with some dimensions of the critical accounting project, there remains much to commend accounting for health. Roslender *et al.* (2006) have suggested that health issues could be an appropriate site for the development of the self-accounting concept. Employee-led health improvement initiatives such as increased sporting activities, walking clubs, aerobics and yoga, as well as healthy eating or smoking cessation programmes, lend themselves to being documented by the participants in their own words, rather than being artificially represented by accountants or other interested management functionaries. Such health 'stories' are conceived of as having greater motivational impact if they come from those directly involved in improving their own health and fitness. As ever, the intranet holds the key to such communications; senior management should make use of it to commit to and encourage health education and promotion.

Summary

The case for identifying workforce health as an element of intellectual capital is based on the observation that health is something that employees, as human capital, bring to the workplace along with their many other attributes. Employers are tasked with at least ensuring that little or nothing that characterises the workplace reduces workforce health and that, wherever possible, it should be enhanced along with employees' other attributes. Current data strongly indicates that the UK, in common with other advanced societies, has a serious work health problem, which is manifested in days lost to sickness. In tandem with taking steps to tackle this problem, it seems desirable to consider how it might be possible to provide some form of account of workforce health. The following chapter documents how this research project was undertaken.

4 RESEARCH DESIGN AND METHOD

Introduction

This chapter initially identifies the broad research questions that were pursued during the empirical parts of the project. Attention then turns to the project's research design and the reasons why a questionnaire survey to both senior accounting and finance and HR directors was chosen as the principal instrument for data collection. Details of the construction of the two samples used for the questionnaire surveys are outlined in the fourth section. The chapter concludes with a brief account of the questionnaire administration process.

Research questions

This study seeks to identify the extent to which senior managers in UK organisations view the health of their workforces as an asset. The researchers come to the study with the conviction that employees are the most important asset that organisations are able to deploy in their value creation and delivery activities; for them, the observation that 'employees are our greatest asset' is more than merely a catchy slogan. It follows that a healthy workforce is a doubly valuable asset, the retention and reproduction of which should be viewed as a strategic imperative for senior managers within organisations. As observed in the previous two chapters, discussions regarding employees as assets have recently been rejuvenated in the context of the increased interest in intellectual capital, where they have been designated human capital, or in the case of Roslender and Fincham (2001, 2004a), primary intellectual capital. In the same way that experience, expertise, commitment or team working capacity are components of human or primary intellectual capital, so too is their health, both being attributes that senior management are continually challenged to grow.

The use of the term 'asset' in the context of employees and their health should immediately signal to accountants that these are aspects of the contemporary organisation that they might consider attempting to 'take into account'. Chapter two briefly outlined the emergence of human asset accounting over 40 years ago, its later evolution into human resource accounting and its subsequent rise and fall as popular accounting research topics. Accounting for intellectual capital has been a relatively well explored avenue within the intellectual capital literature over the past decade or so. Accounting in this context has encompassed two intimately related aspects: a counting or measurement aspect, whether using financial or non-financial (or some combination of both) metrics; and a reporting aspect, where a variety of relevant practices has been identified. For the researchers, workforce health is a further critical phenomenon that accountants might wish to consider measuring and reporting.

It should also be evident from the previous two chapters that the UK has not been in the vanguard of intellectual capital research, at least not in the context of accounting for intellectual capital. One reason for this is a continuing lack of interest in the broader intellectual capital topic in the UK. From the outset, therefore, the researchers held the view that the study was unlikely to uncover an extensive interest in viewing workforce health, envisaged as an element of intellectual capital, as an organisational asset. Nevertheless, they were confident that there would not be a total void in this regard and consequently that it was a valuable exercise to identify what practices are currently in place and attempt to codify these and, if possible, to establish and commend any 'good' practice. As with the previous study of intellectual capital by Fincham and Roslender (2003, 2004; see also Roslender and Fincham, 2004b), this was essentially an exploratory enquiry.

Two questionnaires were developed for the surveys that form the centrepiece of the research - these are reproduced in Appendices One and Two. They reflect the exploratory nature of the enquiry. The first two sections of both questionnaires are identical. Section one was designed to gather information on how respondents viewed workforce health: its importance; monitoring; improvement initiatives; and 'soft' accounting questions on measuring and reporting workforce health. In section two the focus switches to intellectual capital, with questions on how respondents understand the term, their knowledge of approaches to accounting for intellectual capital, and in the case of question 13 their views on how the practice of accounting for intellectual capital is perceived. Section three is concerned with the issues surrounding workforce health as an organisational asset and specifically probes the financial valuation dimension. The questionnaire mailed to accounting and finance directors incorporated an extra section, with questions on the users of accounting information in general and on workforce health in particular, together with a further question (22) on how best to provide information on workforce health to users.

Research design

The decision to use a questionnaire as the principal information gathering tool was taken on the grounds that the research team was seeking to assemble a body of exploratory empirical insights. Despite their many limitations, questionnaires continue to hold out the prospect of providing a breadth of information in return for a relatively modest investment of resources.

In an attempt to counter the perennial problem of a low response rate, the research team planned for the option of two full mailings. The initial mailing occurred in October 2006 and was followed with a second mailing in March 2007. On both occasions a stamped addressed envelope was provided for the return of completed questionnaires (or otherwise). The first mailing produced almost 60% of the total return (297 questionnaires). Inevitably the research team encountered some shrinkage in the potential size of the sample as a result of organisations relocating between October 2006 and March 2007. Overall, the research team conclude that the two full mailings proved very beneficial and should be considered by other research teams intending to use questionnaire surveys for information gathering.

In designing the questionnaires the research team sought to incorporate the opportunity for comment wherever possible. Although it is never possible to replicate the interview situation, a conscious effort was made to gather some further information that would provide a little more depth of insight. It is not possible to say whether this particular attribute of the questionnaires was the reason why a healthy usable response rate (of around 11%) was obtained. It is likely that the use of a second mailing also contributed to the level of response. In addition, the topic itself may have been sufficiently interesting to have prompted a higher than normal response rate. Equally, it should be noted that in the case of many completed questionnaires there was little or no use made of the space left for comments in the questionnaire. Further, only a small number of respondents made use of the opportunity at the end of the questionnaire to provide further comments, although where this did occur, these were normally interesting, if not always positive.

The research team also recognised that it would be desirable to conduct a small number of case studies with organisations that were identified or believed to be in the vanguard of thinking about workforce health as an organisational asset. In due course three organisations were selected to produce a set of case studies that would complement and amplify the findings of the questionnaire surveys.

The questionnaires were designed to provide information of an anonymous nature, with no intention of identifying the source of any specific insights. Nevertheless, a small number of respondents elected to identify their organisation and in some cases provided contact information including business cards, email addresses and telephone numbers. Several returned questionnaires also identified the organisation by means of some procedural technicality such as a dated receipt of enquiry stamp. Unsurprisingly, most of these responses were positive and collectively provided a pool of potential sites for case studies. These leads were followed up by email or by telephone. The three case studies reported in chapter seven were conducted in AstraZeneca, a global pharmaceuticals corporation, South West Water, a utilities provider operating in the south of England and South Lanarkshire Council, a large Scottish local authority. All three were very comfortable with having their organisation's efforts in respect of promoting workforce health identified by name.

The project encompassed surveys of both accounting and finance directors and HR directors. From the outset the project was envisaged as being of a cross-disciplinary nature, pursued by a multi-disciplinary research team, although the accounting dimension is predominant, something that is evident in both questionnaires. The principal focus of the research, workforce health, is an issue that would more commonly be recognised to fall within the sphere of human resource management, as evidenced in the case of long-standing health and safety activities. With the emergence of the intellectual capital field in the mid 1990s, accounting and workforce health have become a little more closely related with each other, particularly in Scandinavia which has traditionally evidenced a more humanistic approach to the management of work and organisations (Johanson et al., 2007). The opportunity to collect information on workforce health from parallel samples of 1,000 accounting and finance directors and HR directors was recognised as a particular strength of the study.

Constructing the sample

The research team set out to identify a sample of organisations that reflected the varied nature of UK businesses. Half of the sample was constituted by the largest 500 UK public limited companies in terms of their number of employees. The source of this sub sample was the Financial Analysis Made Easy (FAME) database (Bureau van Dijk, 2006). Because of their sheer size, such organisations may have strong motivations to be interested in the health of their employees. They also have access to the finance necessary to translate such interests into action, and might, therefore, be considered to be part of the vanguard for employee health promotion. During the recent deliberations about enhancing the Operating and Financial Review, including an element of accounting for people, this category of organisation was, for a time, identified as being mandated to produce such a statement. The database was also used to identify a sub sample of 100 private companies, again using the number of employees as the determining attribute. A third sub sample was constituted by all the listed Scottish companies, at that time 42, principally on the grounds that it might be useful for a Scottish study to collect this information. The sample also included the Top 20 accountancy firms operating in the UK as identified in the June 2006 issue of Accountancy. Together these 662 organisations formed what is referred to in the following pages as the private sector organisations' sub sample.

The largest group of organisations in the public sector and charitable organisations sub sample was constituted by 116 local authorities, including district, borough, town, and city councils. The 100 English and Welsh councils were selected randomly from the local authorities A-Z section of the Improvement and Development Agency for local government (IDeA) website at www.idea-knowledge.gov.uk, together with 16 Scottish local authorities selected randomly from a second website at www.oultwood.com/localgov/countries/scotland.php. A further sample of charitable organisations was also included in this sub sample, the 100 organisations being chosen having the largest number of employees according to details reported in CaritasData's Top 3,000 Charities 2005-6. As Primary Care Trusts presently control 80% of the total budget of the UK National Health Service, it was decided to include within this sub sample 52 English Primary Care Trusts and six Scottish Health Boards. The English websites www.nhs.uk/England/AuthoritiesTrusts/Pct/Default.aspx and its Scottish counterpart www.show.scot.nhs.uk/index.aspx were used to identify this group of organisations. A random group of 50 UK universities was identified using the www.universitiesuk.ac.uk website, with the remaining 14 organisations being a randomly selected group of government agencies chosen from Annex III of the November 2003 *AccountingforPeople Final Report* (DTI, 2003).

Administering the questionnaires

For ease, the questionnaires were mailed to the Director of Finance and the Director of HR respectively, in separate letters. In addition to the appropriate questionnaire, a covering letter briefly setting out the purpose of the research and a request for assistance was included, together with a pre-paid envelope for the return of completed questionnaires. To facilitate the administration of the returned questionnaires and to avoid re-mailing those individuals who had responded to the first mailing, a reference number was discretely handwritten on the reverse side of the return envelope. In the case of the accounting and finance questionnaires these ranged from 1-1,000, with the matching human resource questionnaires being numbered 1,001-2,000. In the covering letter to the second mailing the research team indicated that the numbers on the return envelopes were for administration purposes only. Unfortunately, this did not deter some individuals from disguising their participation, a problem that was again partially rectified.

Returned questionnaires were periodically sorted into the various sub samples identified earlier, with the number on the pre-paid envelope being transferred to the front page of the document. Returns from the second mailing were subject to the same process, being merged with the appropriate sub samples from the first mailing. Details of the sample and response rates are provided in Table 4.1.

Table 4.1   Questionnaire survey responses

Questionnaire survey responses	Number issued	Usable responses			
		Accountancy and finance		Human resources	
	N	N	%	N	%
Private sector organisations					
PLCs	500	42	8.4	36	7.2
Private companies	100	2	2.0	5	5.0
Scottish companies	42	2	4.8	4	9.5
Accountancy firms	20	2	10.0	1	5.0
Total private sector	662	48	7.3	46	6.9
Public sector and charitable organisations					
Local authorities	116	13	11.2	28	24.1
Charities	100	17	17.0	21	21.0
Primary care trusts	58	5	8.6	16	27.6
Universities	50	10	20.0	9	18.0
Government agencies	14	2	14.3	1	7.1
Total public sector and charitable organisations	338	47	13.9	75	22.2
Unidentifiable		4		13	
Total	1,000	99	9.9	134	13.4

In the following two chapters the responses to the questionnaires are reported and discussed, accounting and finance directors in chapter five and HR directors in chapter six. The findings in the three case studies are then reported in chapter seven.

Summary

This study seeks to identify the extent to which senior managers in UK organisations view the health of their workforces as an asset and its resultant reporting. This exploratory study used a questionnaire survey of accounting and finance directors and HR directors. A response rate of 11% was achieved. The findings of the respective surveys are supplemented by three short case studies of leading-edge thinking and practices.

5 ACCOUNTING AND FINANCE DIRECTORS' SURVEY RESPONSES

Introduction

In this chapter the results of the questionnaire survey to the accounting and finance directors are outlined. Initially details of the response profile are presented, followed by the findings in response to the questions contained in the four sections of the questionnaire, designated as: workforce health; intellectual capital; organisational assets; and using accounting information. In the final section of the chapter the main findings of this survey are summarised. The findings are analysed by making use of the composition of the sample, so that any differences between accounting and finance directors employed in the private sector organisations and the public sector and charitable organisations are identified.

Response profile

In total 140 questionnaires were returned by accounting and finance directors, of which 99 provided usable responses. The majority of the unusable responses, 36, were categorisable as 'declined to participate', expressed in a variety of ways, sometimes as a matter of policy, although on occasion dismissing the merits of the questionnaire. Five intended recipients had moved offices. Of the usable responses, 42 were received from public limited companies, which is less than might be expected given the overall structure of the sample. By contrast, 10 responses were received from the 50 universities surveyed, 17 of the 100 charities and 13 of 116 local authorities. The poorest response rate from the accounting and finance directors came from the 100 private companies, with only two completing the questionnaire.

In the case of the HR directors' responses, a total of 157 was received, of which 134 were usable. An initial observation is that of the usable responses from the HR directors, 23 (17.2%) had been returned using the questionnaire mailed to accounting and finance directors. A couple of accounting and finance responses used the human resource management questionnaire, which was far less significant. In all such cases no duplicate returns were received.

Workforce health

The responses of the accounting and finance directors to the initial question, on the importance accorded to physical health within their organisations, are set out in Table 5.1.

Table 5.1   Importance accorded to physical health

Importance accorded to physical health	Private sector organisations		Public sector and charitable organisations		Unidentifiable organisations		Total	
	N	%	N	%	N	%	N	%
A vital consideration	16	33.3	13	27.6	2	50.0	31	31.3
Very important	15	31.3	17	36.2	1	25.0	33	33.3
Important	11	22.9	17	36.2	1	25.0	29	29.3
A minor consideration	6	12.5	-	-	-	-	6	6.1
Total	48	100.0	47	100.0	4	100.0	99	100.0

Including the four unidentifiable respondents, almost two thirds (64.6%) of the accounting and finance directors reported that their organisations viewed physical health as being at least very important, with only six identifying it as unimportant. The application of an appropriate statistical test for this type of categorical variable - the chi-square test of independence - indicates that at the 0.05 level of significance, there would appear to be no association between the type of organisation and level of importance accorded to physical health (test statistic computed as 8.79, with 6 degrees of freedom (df)).

The responses in the case of mental health (Table 5.2) were that 29 viewed it to be a vital consideration while 39 viewed it as being very important. In total over two thirds viewing mental health to be of at least a very important issue.

Table 5.2   Importance accorded to mental health

Importance accorded to mental health	Private sector organisations		Public sector and charitable organisations		Unidentifiable organisations		Total	
	N	%	N	%	N	%	N	%
A vital consideration	12	25.0	14	29.8	3	75.0	29	29.3
Very important	18	37.5	20	42.5	1	25.0	39	39.4
Important	13	27.1	12	25.6	-	-	25	25.3
A minor consideration	5	10.4	1	2.1	-	-	6	6.0
Total	48	100.0	47	100.0	4	100.0	99	100.0

The application of the chi-square test of independence suggest no association between the two variables at the 0.05 significance level (test statistic: 7.55; df 6).

Only a minority of respondents provided any comments on their responses to these initial questions. In one of the primary care trusts, having observed that the organisation considers physical health to be an important issue, a respondent observed that:

[I]*t should be viewed higher. Unfortunately there is always too much organisational change to allow us the time to develop workforce health initiatives properly.*

Respondents in two of the charitable organisations commented that, because of the nature of the work involved, a high level of physical fitness was important, something echoed in a response from a construction industry respondent who took the view that very high levels of physical health were a 'high priority'. A respondent from a finance industry organisation identified why high levels of physical health were critical in this organisation:

We have a very small team and we do not wish them to be distracted with health worries.

Similar sentiments were expressed by a respondent from a second public limited company, who commented that:

We are a people business. Our assets are our people.

Overall, however, only a very minimal level of comment was evident in the case of mental health, with the most expansive observation, from a local authority based respondent, betraying a somewhat sceptical tone:

The organisation values it [mental wellbeing] *but it doesn't resource it sufficiently highly.*

The next question sought information on the extent of arrangements designed to monitor workforce health. Table 5.3 indicates that at present these arrangements largely remain moderate.

Table 5.3   Provision for monitoring workforce health

Provision for monitoring workforce health	Private sector organisations		Public sector and charitable organisations		Unidentifiable organisations		Total	
	N	%	N	%	N	%	N	%
Extensive	9	18.8	8	17.0	-	-	17	17.2
Moderate	26	54.1	28	59.6	3	75.0	57	57.6
Rudimentary	9	18.8	11	23.4	1	25.0	21	21.2
None	4	8.3	-	-	-	-	4	4.0
Total	48	100.0	47	100.0	4	100.0	99	100.0

Overall, the extent of health monitoring seems to be lower than might be hoped for, given the importance claimed for employee health in chapter three. Conversely, these findings are largely consistent with those reported in Table 5.1 and 5.2, where less than a third of respondents indicated that either physical or mental health was a vital consideration at this time. The same conclusion applies in the case of the chi-square test of independence for Table 5.3 - with no apparent association between type of organisation and response (test statistic: 5.62; df 6).

Comments on monitoring workforce health were more extensive. In the public sector and charitable organisations sub sample, many respondents identified the existence of sickness and/or absence monitoring procedures, frequently combined with a system of return to work interviews. The latter were commonly linked to referrals to occupational health departments for 'problem' cases and intervention where necessary. In some organisations similar activities were evident but on a less formal basis, with managers tasked with raising sickness or absence issues, where necessary, with staff at annual performance reviews. Again, the facility to refer individuals to occupational health seemed to be in place, although perhaps on a more ad hoc basis. A number of respondents identified the existence of pre-employment health checks for new starters. In a small number of organisations, arrangements existed to monitor the health of all employees on regular basis, usually annually. A variation on this arrangement was reported in one case with senior managers undergoing regular BUPA health checks, while their subordinates had access to separate medical insurance schemes.

The following are examples of more comprehensive provisions being in place, the first in a government agency, the second in a charity:

> *There is a computerised e-absence system with formal return to work interviews which are evidenced. HR reviews this information to identify persistent 'small' sick absences. Referral to Occupational Health happens where there is prolonged absence. We also have periodic health check-ups, with frequency proportionate to absence.*

> *Absences from work are all monitored. These include sickness which has to be formally reported to line managers who sign off sickness forms which are returned to HR. Both HR and payroll are able to produce reports on absence.*

It is noteworthy that the first respondent believed arrangements were currently only moderate, while the second identified them as being rudimentary.

There was a distinct difference in the comments offered by respondents in the private sector organisations. The principal approach to monitoring workforce health was identified as being through various health screening procedures. Some of these were performed in-house, either by an occupational health specialist or by qualified medical personnel, whose services were sometimes available on a continuing basis. A sizeable number of organisations reported that staff had access to health care schemes, with senior employees being particularly well looked after. The following observations were reasonably typical where such arrangements were in place:

All senior managers have a full annual medical, and access to free private health care. All staff has access to subsidised health care and, through a confidential employee counselling service, can discuss their personal health concerns.

Provisions for sickness monitoring combined with return to work interviews and referrals where necessary were also identified but not as extensively as in the case of the other sub sample. One respondent expressed reservations about the value of such arrangements:

We have a system for reporting sickness and absence. This is an unreliable method for monitoring health as many employees falsely report absence due to sickness for short term periods.

Finally, one respondent indicated that the arrangement in place within her/his organisation was 'common sense', which presumably means it is the responsibility of individuals to manage their own personal health.

Over half of the respondents - 53 - believed that their organisations had taken some steps to improve the health of their workforces. Table 5.4 indicates that the public sector and charitable organisations were more advanced than those in the private sector, with all four unidentifiable respondents reporting a better than average position within their various organisations.

Table 5.4   Steps taken to improve workforce health

Steps taken to improve workforce health	Private sector organisations		Public sector and charitable organisations		Unidentifiable organisations		Total	
	N	%	N	%	N	%	N	%
Some	20	41.7	29	61.7	4	100.0	53	53.5
Few	17	35.4	13	27.7	-	-	30	30.3
None	11	22.9	5	10.6	-		16	16.2
Total	48	100.0	47	100.0	4	100.0	99	100.0

In the case of these responses, while there would again appear to be no association between the two variables (test statistic: 8.09; df 4) at the 0.05 level of significance, this would not be the case at the 0.10 level of significance.

A variety of initiatives were identified by respondents. In the public sector and charitable organisations respondents most commonly identified encouraging employees to take up sporting and kindred activities, often at free or subsidised gymnasia, as well as lunchtime walks, walking to work or in one case by providing a free loan of bikes. Encouraging employees to stop smoking, whether by the introduction of smoking bans or by means of support groups was regularly mentioned. Health promotion activities, including specific health initiatives, health days and providing flu vaccinations, were organised in some cases, as were the provision of 'healthy eating' menus and free fruit. One organisation had also introduced healthy cooking lessons for employees. BUPA memberships, a stress survey, free eye tests, ergonomic assessments of work sites and reduced working hours were also subscribed to in specific cases.

A broader range of initiatives was reported by the private sector organisations' respondents, with an emphasis on health and safety programmes and the provision of health care facilities being the most widely supported. Smoking bans were less evident as were healthy menus. There was also a reasonable level of support for sports activities with evidence of some inventiveness, for example, the provision of a yoga class at lunchtimes, a cycling competition, a self-explanatory 10,000 step initiative and the introduction of netball sessions for female staff. One organisation was particularly adventurous:

> *The 'Get a Life' scheme focuses on allowing employees one experience each year they'd not normally undertake. There is also some health screening and we have tried to develop a quality office environment. Over-stressed people don't perform. An optimal level of 'stress' is required for motivational purposes.*

At the other end of the spectrum was the respondent who answered that the organisation had taken no steps to either monitor or improve the health of its workforce, adding:

> [A]*lthough having a gym in our new offices might make a difference.*

Unfortunately it was not possible to determine whether this constituted a wish or an expectation!

Question six was the first accounting orientated question, asking whether any attempt was being made to measure the health of workforces. The same findings were evident in the two identifiable sub samples, with fewer than a third reporting some attempt to measure workforce health: 29.2% in the case of the private sector companies and 31.9% in the other sub sample. None of the four unidentifiable organisations attempted measurement. The local authorities, perhaps not surprisingly given the responses to the previous question, reported being more advanced in measuring health, in 6 of 13 instances (46.2%). By comparison only 12 of the 42 (28.6%) public limited companies were presently involved in measuring workforce health. A couple of these respondents offered some insights on measurement in their accompanying comments:

Summary reports are provided by BUPA on the health screening programmes which they run for us. Health programmes are reported to the Centre every 6 months, with numbers and type. We also report on occupational illnesses every three months. Our UK EAP [Employee Assistance programme] *also provides monthly reports.*

A similar comprehensive approach to measuring the health of the workforce was identified by a second public limited company:

The People Management Initiative measures many things: attendance; reasons for absence; medical or ambulance call outs for employees; sent home stats and reasons for these actions; workplace H&S [Health and Safety] *activity on lifting, seating and screen usage.*

In the case of the complementary accounting practice of reporting on workforce health, the responses diverged less. Overall, 45 (45.4%) organisations claimed that they reported on workforce health. However, there was a marked difference between the private sector organisations and the public sector and charitable organisations. In only 18 (37.5%) of the private sector organisations was reporting claimed, while 26 of 47 (55.3%) public sector and charitable organisation respondents claimed that they did so. Once again the local authority responses suggest that such organisations are in the vanguard, with nine of the 13 authorities (69.2%) reporting on workforce health, to a variety of stakeholders including the senior (corporate) management team, 'the Cabinet', elected members, employment committees, and in some cases to senior departmental managers. Both of the government agencies claimed that they reported on workforce health to their respective Management Boards, together with three of the five primary care trusts, albeit to unidentified stakeholders. The universities appeared to be laggards, although in one instance it was intimated that an absence monitoring reporting system was currently under development, while in the private sector organisations the two accountancy firms also claimed to be reporting on workforce health, in one case to a Health and Safety Committee.

The final question in this section sought to elicit responses on any proposals to make workforce health a more important consideration in the future. The responses to this question were very disappointing, with only 21 (21.2%) respondents reporting that such proposals were currently being considered. The position in both principal sub samples was almost identical with only marginally more than a fifth reporting that workforce health was likely to become a greater consideration. Once again the local authorities appeared to be the most progressive, with 5 of the 13 organisations (38.5%) indicating positive change. In one organisation:

Improved employee healthcare facilities are being developed. Processes for improving recruitment are being reviewed, although for selected groups these have been initially identified as not being cost effective. There are also plans for more active referrals for absent employees to the healthcare team.

By contrast, among the charities only a single organisation reported that improvements might occur in the future, with the universities reporting this in 30% of cases. A respondent from one of the primary care trusts was clearly less enthusiastic about the future:

There has been massive organisational change recently, with maybe more to come. It will be years before anyone gets around to thinking properly about workforce health.

In summary, the responses to this first set of questions suggest that there is little reason for optimism that workforce health either is or is about to become a major issue within UK organisations, at least not among senior accounting and finance managers.

Intellectual capital

The responses to the question about familiarity with the terms 'intellectual capital' or 'intangibles' were encouraging, given the findings of Roslender and Fincham's 2003 study. Of the 99 responses, 84 (84.8%) indicated that they were at least familiar with these terms and only 12 (12.1%) unfamiliar. Table 5.5 indicates that private sector sub sample claimed to be better appraised than their counterparts.

Table 5.5   Familiarity with the terms 'intellectual capital' or 'intangibles'

Familiarity with the terms 'intellectual capital' or 'intangibles'	Private sector organisations		Public sector and charitable organisations		Unidentifiable organisations		Total	
	N	%	N	%	N	%	N	%
Very familiar	24	50.0	16	34.0	2	50.0	42	42.4
Familiar	19	39.6	22	46.9	1	25.0	42	42.4
Have heard of them	1	2.1	1	2.1	1	25.0	3	3.1
Unfamiliar	4	8.3	8	17.0	-	-	12	12.1
Total	48	100.0	47	100.0	4	100.0	99	100.0

Once again at the 0.05 level of significance, there would appear to be no association between the type of organisation and the extent of familiarity (test statistic: 10.7; df 6); however at the next level up (0.10), the conclusion becomes less robust.

Within the public sector and charitable organisations, familiarity was reported to be greatest among the respondents in the charitable organisations, with 47.1% being very familiar and 41.2% being familiar, and lowest in the case of the local authorities, with 15.4% and 69.2% respectively. The highest report of a lack of familiarity came, perhaps surprisingly, from the 10 university respondents, of whom four claimed to be unfamiliar with the terms.

The variety of understandings of these terms is instructive. One respondent from a public limited company suggested a definition of intellectual capital in the following terms:

These two expressions are not the same thing. In the context of this survey 'IC' is the unquantified value that an organisation possesses that is locked up in its staff, as a result of the way it conducts its business. It is 'knowledge', 'technique', 'implementation', 'expertise'.

A second clarified this distinction:

Intangibles are assets without physical substance e.g. R&D, licenses, etc. Intellectual capital is the talent, training and professional skills of a workforce.

The position embraced by one of the accountancy firm respondents was very narrowly focused:

Relates to fields of I.S., innovation research and technology transfer where the 'brain power' of certain individuals is assigned a value. Relates closely to concepts of copyright and patents.

By contrast a respondent from a primary care trust advanced a more holistic understanding:

Intellectual capital is the knowledge, skills and understanding acquired by an organisation that enables it to improve its performance relative to those organisations without it. It therefore has value. Intangibles are assets that cannot be seen or touched but nevertheless improve the organisation's ability to generate profits.

The performance nexus was affirmed by a respondent from a charitable organisation:

Qualities in an individual or group of individuals which affect performance.

Finally, in one of the unidentifiable organisations, both aspects of asset and performance are brought together:

An intangible is some asset that has no physical substance. Intellectual capital is an intangible that gives a business competitive advantage.

Overall, it seems reasonable to conclude that although familiarity with these terms is relatively high, this is not to be confused with a detailed understanding of their meaning and significance.

Question 11 asked how familiar respondents were with attempts to account for intellectual capital such as the Balanced Scorecard or the Intellectual Capital Statement. The responses in this case were less positive with marginally fewer than half, 49, of the total sample indicating awareness of some developments but 41 (41.4%) being unaware of such developments. The remaining nine respondents claimed to be very familiar with these developments. Of these, five were from public limited companies and one from an accountancy firm. By contrast only a single respondent in the public sector and charitable organisations claimed to be very familiar with these developments. In the case of the respondents from the universities, six claimed awareness of some developments, seemingly contradicting their responses to question nine on familiarity with the term intellectual capital. In the local authority sub sample, eight (61.5%) indicated that they were unfamiliar with such developments.

The final question in this section of the questionnaire asked how important respondents thought it was to incorporate intellectual capital within financial statements. Overall, the most common response to this question was that this was of only minor importance, a view expressed by 37 (37.4%) respondents. A distraction was the view held by 29 (29.3%) of respondents, some of whom were very dismissive in their accompanying comments:

Accounts should be about historical cost, not academic theory a la IFRS.

Arguably extremely hard to measure, usually non-transferable and of little benefit to the users of financial statements.

Don't go there. A waste of time.

All three observations were from respondents in private sector organisations. Twenty eight respondents thought it was quite important to attempt to incorporate it. Only five respondents indicated that this was a very important matter, a finding that would seem to support the general conclusion that intellectual capital still does not appear to be a major issue for large numbers within the UK accountancy profession. The following are presently the views of a small minority, the first from a charitable organisation, the second from a public limited company respondent:

> *Human assets can walk away with their intellectual capital.*

> *They [IC] are a key asset of any company or group which is not often prescribed a value at present.*

Among the two principal sub samples, 18 respondents believed that this issue was of only minor importance in each case. On balance, the public sector and charitable organisations' respondents were more positive, reporting that intellectual capital was either a very important or quite an important issue in 17 (36.2%) cases. This compared with 14 (29.2%) of the private sector organisations' respondents. Conversely, 16 (33.3%) private sector organisations regarded it as a distraction, with 12 (25.5%) holding this view within the other sub sample. Charitable organisations and the universities were again the more enthusiastic respondents, the former returning very favourable views, while the local authorities were least attracted by the issues involved.

Organisational assets

The initial question in the third section of the questionnaire asked whether respondents believed that workforce health qualifies as an organisational asset. The sample as a whole agreed that this was the case but only just, with 51 (51.5%) respondents taking this view. The sub sample of respondents from the public sector and charitable organisations disagreed, again only marginally, 24 (24.2%) saying no. Both of the government agency respondents held this view, as did nine of the 17 charitable organisations. The comments offered in response to this question were quite varied. Having answered negatively, a respondent from one of the charitable organisations then continued:

> *It depends on the workforce. If as an organisation you employ largely casual and part time staff who are easily recruited then they cease to be an organisational asset.*

A number of respondents enrolled commonsense accounting criteria:

> *Difficult to place a value on it that wouldn't be subjective. You need clear guidelines to work with.*

> *Not in accounting terms. Not a fixed asset properly guaranteed to last for more than one accounting period.*

> *It would be too subjective to quantify and distorts from the true meaning of the figures.*

Having responded yes to question 14, another respondent continued:

> *Whilst intangible, good health is an asset from which revenue can be generated. Arguably good health may not be considered an asset, rather an assumption, while poor health is a liability.*

The greatest support for viewing workforce health as an asset was provided in the case of the public limited companies, where 25 (59.5%)

offered a positive response to this question. This was out of step with the broader sample, as well as with the two private companies and two private accountancy firms, both of which answered no to this question, with the two Scottish companies responding yes and no. Arguably the most positive response, from a public limited company, asserted that:

> *Thirty per cent of the costs in* [this company] *are people. One hundred per cent of the value of* [this company] *is people - our staff.*

At the opposite end of the continuum, a respondent from a private company commented dismissively that:

> *Temporary staff can always cover for absenteeism.*

Some of the implications of viewing workforces and their health as assets were evident in several responses including the following pair from public limited company respondents:

> *I believe that it is an asset in that a workforce is an asset of a business, so clearly a healthy workforce is better than an unhealthy workforce. However, I don't believe that it may be included as an asset in financial statements.*
>
> *It is normal for organisations to have employees in various states of health. I do not believe you can treat the health of an employee as an asset without treating the employee as an asset. This is not a path I would like to go down.*

Again at the extreme, a further respondent commented simply: 'No requirement for plc reporting.'.

In question 16, accounting and finance directors were asked whether it is possible to place a financial value on workforce health. Less than half the respondents (44) believed that it was possible to do this. The distribution of positive responses was interesting; 25 (53.2%) of the public sector and charitable organisations sub sample took the view that it was possible to place a financial value on workforce health compared with only 17 (35.4%) of private sector organisations' respondents. Among the public sector and charitable organisations, nine local authority respondents took this view, having previously reported that it was not possible to view workforce health as an organisational asset.

Once again some of the reasoning was insightful. Having answered 'yes' to question 16, a local authority respondent continued:

> *It is possible to cost the impact of non-attendance and hence quantify the impact of bad health. The problem would be, however, in costing the baseline of underlying illness e.g. colds, flu, etc., and non-work related problems e.g. cancer.*

A charitable organisation respondent boldly announced that:

> *Everything can be valued. The important issue is having a consistent basis that either you use to benchmark yourself or everyone i.e. other companies, uses so that you can benchmark each other.*

Conversely one of the public limited company respondents believed that:

> *It would be very difficult to form a view on a fixed value for such an intangible but that in itself shouldn't prevent it from being done.*

A respondent from one of the unidentifiable organisations thought it better not to pursue this issue arguing:

It is too esoteric. I could place a value of £100K on it but on what basis? Someone else could place another value on it. Year on year, across a workforce, health remains fairly constant. Better not to value.

Another public sector organisation respondent distinguished between health and ill health, answering no on the grounds that:

We could cost up sickness absence but that is ill health, not health.

Finally, for a significant number of respondents across the whole sample the answer was rather obvious and could be paraphrased as: 'no because any value would necessarily be subjective and, as a consequence, not reliable'.

Question 17 offered respondents a number of possible designations for workforce health as an asset. Table 5.6 indicates that the responses to this question were somewhat at odds with those received in the case of question 14.

Table 5.6   Asset designation of workforce health

Asset designation of workforce health	Private sector organisations		Public sector and charitable organisations		Unidentifiable organisations		Total	
	N	%	N	%	N	%	N	%
Tangible asset	-	-	1	2.1	-	-	1	1.0
Intangible asset	11	22.9	8	17.0	2	50.0	21	21.2
Operational asset	6	12.5	10	21.3	-	-	16	16.2
Human asset	27	56.3	23	48.9	2	50.0	52	52.5
None of these	4	8.3	5	10.7	-	-	9	9.1
Total	48	100.0	47	100.0	4	100.0	99	100.0

The public sector and charitable organisations sub sample lagged a little behind the private sector organisations in relation to the human asset designation, with 48.9% support compared with 56.3%. Among the former sub sample the charitable organisations' respondents took this view in 10 of the 17 (58.8%) cases. This compares with 23 of the 42 responses (54.8%) from the public limited companies. Twenty one (21.2%) respondents viewed workforce health as an intangible asset, while 16 (16.2%) viewed it as an operational asset, ten of whom were from the public sector and charitable organisations sub sample. The chi-square test of independence once again suggests no association between these two variables at the 0.05 significance level (test statistic: 5.56; df 8).

Only a minority of respondents volunteered further reflections on this question. A primary care trust respondent who had previously answered that it was possible to place a financial valuation on workforce health commented:

It's clearly an intangible asset as you can't see or touch it. But it is a human asset because it's human in nature and is part of the workforce. In my opinion human assets should be a sub-set of intangibles but I still think it is inappropriate to carry a value in the balance sheet.

One of the public limited company respondents also made a link with the valuation issue:

I can no more quantify a 'healthy' workforce than a hard working one; or a workforce of higher intellect or ethics. So I see 'health' in the round context of the human asset, not a stand alone one.

Viewing workforce health as an operational asset, a second public limited company respondent continued:

Because it would be reflected in operational results. Too transient to be capitalised but you could argue that it is akin to professional footballers, who are capitalised and adjusted according to useful economic life. So not an original concept.

Other respondents were more pragmatic, as in the case of one who identified workforce health as an intangible asset because 'it fits the definition given in Q9'.

The final question in this section follows logically from the previous four, and provides some indication of how respondents believed it might be possible to account for workforce health in the absence of being able to derive a simple financial valuation for this particular type of asset (Table 5.7)

Table 5.7   Means of accounting for workforce health

Means of accounting for workforce health	Private sector organisations		Public sector and charitable organisations		Unidentifiable organisations		Total	
	N	%	N	%	N	%	N	%
Financial measures	3	6.3	-	-	-	-	3	3.0
Substitute financial measures	1	2.1	5	10.6	-	-	6	6.2
Non-financial measures	15	31.2	7	14.9	2	50.0	24	24.2
Narrative approach	10	20.8	12	25.5	2	50.0	24	24.2
Some combination of the above	18	37.5	21	44.7	-	-	39	39.4
Other means	1	2.1	2	4.3	-	-	3	3.0
Total	48	100.0	47	100.0	4	100.0	99	100.0

At the 0.05 level of significance there appears to be no association between the type of organisation and responses on the means of accounting for workforce health (test statistic: 13.9; df 10)

Initially, a small number of respondents (3) indicated that irrespective of what was being explored in this question, only traditional financial numbers were appropriate. They might be designated as a hardcore of practitioners who have little sympathy with anything beyond the narrowest interpretation of accounting and reporting. Six respondents identified using substitute financial measures to achieve this objective, five of whom came from the public sector and charitable organisations sub sample. In the case of the other two one-dimensional options identified, support was the same for the use of some type of non-financial measures or a narrative approach to accounting for workforce health, both in 24 (24.2%) cases. Within the former group, 15 were from the public limited companies sub sample, including the following respondent who raised the following accounting poser:

Better to use a measure such as days lost as a % of total days. If a day is valued, would it be at the cost to the business or price to the customer as opportunity cost?

Only the university respondents offered any further sizeable support for this option. Support for the use of narrative information alone to achieve this objective was expressed across the sample. Strong support for narratives was expressed by a respondent from one of the unidentifiable organisations, who also offered the following critique of a measurement perspective:

It's the only straight forward method that doesn't waste effort. The thought process in creating narrative is more likely to focus the mind on any issues than measurement does. Measurement tends to bring most focus to bear on how the measurement is performed than on the actual results.

It is perhaps unsurprising that the greatest support was offered for the use of some combination of substitute financial, non-financial and narrative information. This was the view of 39 (39.4%) of respondents. There was marginally more support for this approach evident within the public sector and charitable organisations, 21 of 47 cases, with enthusiasm particularly evident among this sub sample of charitable organisations. By comparison, only 18 of the respondents from the other principal sub sample supported this approach, with just a third of respondents (14) from the public limited companies taking this view. Overall, given the level of support for this option and the same level of support for the narrative and non-financial measures options, there is evidence to conclude that a significant number of accounting practitioners may be becoming more enthusiastic about a multi-dimensional approach to financial reporting, in which numbers are used in combination with an appropriate narrative content.

Three respondents identified the use of 'other means' of accounting for workforce health. Two identified vaguely narrative approaches, one talking about reporting workforce health in a separate document alongside the social and charitable activities pursued by the organisation. The other took the view that such information should be incorporated into some form of 'off-balance sheet' report, presumably by means of narrative information. A further respondent simply answered 'who knows', which in some respects might be taken as a reflection of the general view of this particular sample of respondents.

Using accounting information

The initial question in the fourth section of the questionnaire asked who respondents viewed as the principal users of the accounting information that they produced. Two contrasting profiles were evident. In the case of the public sector and charitable organisations the government was identified as the principal user, in 33 (70.2%) cases, followed by the general public in 27 (57.4%) cases and employees in

25 (53.2%) cases. The next highest was the 'other' category, which was identified in 17 (36.2%) cases. In the case of the charities, five respondents identified donors as being important users, while in the universities users included the University Court and alumni.

The private sector respondents identified analysts as the principal users, in 42 (87.5%) cases, marginally ahead of shareholders and lenders, both in 39 (81.3%) cases. Employees were the next most cited user, in 18 (37.5%) cases, very different from the profile evident in the public sector and charitable organisations sub sample. The general public attracted support in nine (18.8%) cases. In addition, several further users were mentioned including the Financial Services Authority, regulators, local government and in two cases, customers. The profile of responses among the four unidentifiable organisations was closer to the private sector organisations than the other sub sample.

Respondents were then asked which of these users might have an interest in accounting information on workforce health. In the case of the public sector and charitable organisations, employees, the government and the general public were again identified as the principal stakeholders who might be interested in accounting information on workforce health. Employees were identified as being most likely to be interested in having such information available, in 28 (59.6%) cases, followed by the government and the general public in 20 (41.7%) and 18 (38.3) cases respectively. As with question 19, relatively few respondents added any further commentary. Having identified the government as being interested in accounting information on workforce health, a respondent in a university commented:

A significant level of funding is received by the University from the government.

A local authority respondent commented that such interest was the result of:

The view of 'value for money' and comparisons with other organisations, although it is probably more of 'periodic curiosity'.

The view of one charitable organisation respondent was that:

Employees would inevitably be interested in the organisation's attitudes to their health.

A second local authority respondent only identified employees adding the observation:

It's there (sic) health.

Among the 'other' prospective users, the trade unions were identified by a couple of respondents, reinforcing its perceived importance to employees.

Fewer users were identified in responses to this question than to the previous question (19), a pattern replicated in the private sector organisations sub sample. For these respondents, employees were again identified as the users who might be interested in receiving information on workforce health, in 30 (62.5%) cases, which exceeds the level evident in the case of the public sector and charitable organisations. Shareholders and analysts were the next most identified groups, in 22 (45.8%) and 20 (41.7%) cases respectively, roughly half the levels for the previous question. Lenders were not perceived to be greatly interested in such information being identified in only 11 (22.9%) cases. Interest attributed to the general public and the government was low compared with the public sector and charitable organisations, in nine and six cases respectively.

A number of respondents identified the reasons for the interest of many users in some detail, as in the case of this public limited company respondent:

Company shareholders and analysts are interested in the impact of health on company performance. Employees are directly interested. Government is interested to see the impact of National Health Service policies on business results and therefore wider economic performance.

A further important observation on the responses to question 20 is that several respondents expressed the view that nobody was interested in receiving such information, doing so rather pointedly in some cases. This might also be the view of the further, sizeable group of respondents who failed to provide any answer to this question.

Question 22 focused on the means of providing information on workforce health to interested users. While similar to question 18, this question incorporated further options, and being placed later in the questionnaire was intended to promote greater reflection on the issues under enquiry. The most popular mechanism now identified was some form of non-financial report (narrative) supplementary to the financial statements, reported in 36 cases. Support for such an approach was significantly greater in the public sector and charitable organisations, in 20 cases, compared with 14 cases in the other sub sample. Detailed reasoning was unfortunately rather scarce, although where provided proved instructive:

I do not believe that non-financial information such as this should be included in the financial statements.

While we consider workforce health to be important so are a number of other areas which also require monitoring on a regular basis. We have KPIs for these areas and I would include workforce health within these.

I think the topic best fits with corporate responsibility. I also think it is more likely to be seen as few people read accounts. I also believe that it is confusing to users when financial statements include non-financial information.

Background information. Not the real raison d'etre for being interested in an organisation.

Cannot place a financial value in a consistent, comparable way, therefore financial reporting is not valid. How would it be audited?

The next most popular were the two combination options (3 and 6). While the public sector and charitable organisations favoured an approach that combined financial data and narratives as a supplement to the financial statements (option 6), the private sector organisations preferred financial data combined with narratives within the financial statements (option 3). A respondent from one of the primary care trusts set out the reasoning for electing to combine financial data with non-financial data within the financial statements:

I think workforce health is best measured through a combination of financial and non-financial measures. It is important to disclose it as well as other aspects of the workforce e.g. diversity, age, turnover, etc. I believe that information has to be part of the financial statements to carry any weight. I'm not convinced that corporate social responsibility reports have a sufficient level of importance.

The opposite view was expressed by a private sector organisation respondent:

It's not solid enough to form part of normal financial statements.

When support for the latter alternatives was combined, 34 (34.3%) respondents indicated their support for some form of compromise, which is only slightly less than the level of support for the use of supplementary narratives only. It might also be noted that three further respondents specifically identified a stand alone staff (employee) report as the most appropriate means of providing workforce health information, with a further respondent identifying the corporate social responsibility report as being the appropriate vehicle.

Irrespective of the responses to question 18 previously documented, very little support was expressed for an approach that reported financial data, either within the financial statements, in three cases, or supplementary to the financial statements. Respondents, particularly those in the private sector organisations were rather more attracted to the use of a narrative approach within the context of the financial statements, in ten cases, including the following enthusiast for the recently introduced Business Review model:

As part of the Business Review narrative reporting, a number of employee measures will appear as KPIs in narrative reports such as utilisation, staff turnover. If these measures benchmark v competitors are good, no other KPIs will be needed. If they don't then directors may use other measures to explain trends.

Finally, four respondents took the view that there was no need for providing this sort of information, having been generally sceptical about it throughout their responses. Three of these were from the public limited companies.

The penultimate question asked whether respondents were aware of initiatives elsewhere in the world designed to account for workforce health. Had they any knowledge of what was going on in Scandinavia, for example? Only a single respondent, employed by a charitable organisation, answered affirmatively, having become familiar with the use of Intellectual Capital Statements during employment in Australia. This perfectly highlights the lack of understanding in the UK about how it might be possible to account for intellectual capital in general, and workforce health in particular.

The final question (24) sought to solicit any further comments. On balance, those who responded were critical of the project:

> *Financial statements and disclosure requirements under IFRS and the Combined Code are already a serious burden to business and have resulted in unreadable reports and accounts. Any further additions and complications will only exacerbate the situation. Let's keep life simple, please.*

> *Accounts should not include any further items that lead to misunderstanding or additional bureaucracy with little or no benefit, such as workforce health and intellectual capital.*

> *I seem to be averse to the project's assumption that more employer action and reporting is desirable. My general view is we have the NHS for health and should not duplicate, taking resources out of teaching and research.*

> *If this survey will be used to impose yet another disclosure, I thoroughly depreciate (sic) it.*

> *This would be a total waste of time.*

A minority were insightful:

> *How can workforce health be measured? We can measure or report on absence claimed to be caused by poor health but without full medical examinations how do we know the health status of each employee?*

> *I am clearly influenced by our business which is investment, where the balance sheet is at fair value and 'staff' value is not a major*

factor in how we are seen e.g. pension liability = 0.05% of net assets. We trade at a discount to net assets which is arguably (I wouldn't) a negative management premium.

And one respondent was most supportive:

Interesting questionnaire - look forward to results.

Summary

The above responses suggest that UK accounting and finance directors believe that both the physical and mental health of the workforce are currently viewed as being a vital consideration in only a minority of organisations. The numbers reporting that mental health is viewed as a very important issue were greater, especially in the public sector and charitable organisations. A modest 58% of respondents reported that it is possible to identify the existence of arrangements for monitoring workforce health in their organisations, with no discernible difference between the two sub samples in this case.

The principal monitoring mechanism was that of sickness or absence records in the case of the public sector and charitable organisations, with private sector organisations more reliant on the outcome of health screening arrangements. The responses received suggest that the public sector and charitable organisations are more involved in seeking to promote workforce health, with the local authorities in the vanguard in almost 80% of cases. Among the private sector organisations, a sizeable number reported no provisions had yet been made. No particular initiative seemed to be widely pursued.

Beyond collecting absence data, there seemed to be little interest in measuring workforce health, with private sector respondents less disposed to action. There was greater interest in reporting on work health, however, with 55% of public sector and charitable organisations claiming to do so (69% in the case of the local authorities), and 38% among the private sector organisations. The largely unencouraging picture of relatively limited interest in workforce health was confirmed as only a little over 20% of respondents indicated that plans were currently in place to make workforce health a more important consideration in the future. The responses from the local authorities suggest that these organisations are the most enthusiastic about these issues.

An unexpectedly high number of respondents (85%) claimed to be either familiar or very familiar with the term intellectual capital, with the private sector organisations' sub sample claiming even higher levels. In contrast to this, and perhaps surprisingly, four of the ten university sector respondents were unfamiliar with this term. Knowledge of how to account for intellectual capital was much less widespread, however, with only 59% indicating some awareness of the options presently available. The Balanced Scorecard was the most widely identified means of doing this. Private sector organisations seemed better appraised of such developments, with less than 40% of local authority respondents familiar with such developments. Two thirds of the sample took the view that, at best, attempting to incorporate intellectual capital within financial statements was of minor importance, with 29 respondents taking the view that it constituted a distraction. The public sector and charitable organisations were marginally more supportive of the practice, 36% of respondents believing it to be either a very important or a quite important issue.

Just over half (52%) of respondents agreed with the view that workforce health qualifies as an organisational asset. The greatest support was evident among public limited company respondents, in almost 60% of cases. This was noticeably different from the rest of the broader private sector organisations sub sample, however, with the public sector and charitable organisations being more or less evenly divided in their views on the assertion. The latter sub sample responded similarly to the question on the possibility of placing a financial value on workforce health, 53% being in agreement, although a significantly greater (69%) degree of support was voiced by local authority respondents. Only 35% of private sector organisations took this view, with the result that overall only 44% of respondents believed it was possible to identify a financial value for workforce health.

Workforce health was identified as a human asset in 53% of cases, 21% of respondents viewing it as an intangible asset. A single respondent took the view that it was a tangible asset. In the absence of financial valuations, 24% of respondents advocated the use of non-financial measures, while a further 24% suggested the use of narrative reporting. Only a minority considered the development of substitute financial measures to be appropriate. The greatest support was offered for some combination of all three approaches, in 39% of responses, with a greater level of enthusiasm for such an approach evident among the public sector and charitable organisations sub sample. A narrative approach was also identified by a number of those who suggested other means of reporting. Only financial valuations would satisfy the needs of a tiny minority.

The responses to the question on the principal users of financial information are very different. For those in the private sector organisations it is analysts closely followed by shareholders and lenders, all in excess of 80%. By contrast, the public sector and charitable organisations' respondents identified the government as the principal user in 70% of cases, some way ahead of the general public and employees, the only other users to score in excess of 50%. Both principal sub samples agreed that employees are likely to be the most interested in receiving information on workforce health, with the private sector organisation respondents marginally in the vanguard, at 63% as compared with 60%. By contrast, a number of respondents suggested that nobody is interested in receiving this sort of information.

Responses also indicated that some form of supplementary narrative was considered as the most appropriate way to provide information on workforce health to users, albeit in only a little over of a third of cases overall, with more support from public sector and charitable organisation respondents. This was a marginal preference, however, with only two fewer respondents identifying a combination of numbers and narrative. In the case of their private sector counterparts, the preference was for a combination of numbers and narrative incorporated within financial statements. Finally, only a single respondent was aware of existing attempts to account for intellectual capital.

6 HUMAN RESOURCE DIRECTORS' SURVEY RESPONSES

Introduction

In this chapter the results of the questionnaire survey to the HR directors are outlined. Because the questionnaire used for this survey differed a little from that used in the case of the accounting and finance directors, the centrepiece of the chapter is constituted by three rather than four sections on: workforce health; intellectual capital; and organisational assets. As in the previous chapter, the following analysis is informed by the composition of the sample. Initially details of the response profile are provided and the chapter concludes with a summary of the main findings of this survey.

Response profile

The HR directors returned a total of 157 completed questionnaires, which was proportionately higher than their counterparts from accounting and finance. Of these, 134 were usable, a notably higher proportion than for their counterparts. Twelve of the unusable responses were the result of intended recipients having moved offices, the remaining 11 declining to participate for similar reasons to accounting and finance directors. As observed in the previous chapter, of the usable responses from the HR directors, 23 (17.2%) were returned using the questionnaire mailed to accounting and finance directors. Taken together, these preliminary observations suggest that HR directors were more disposed to the study than colleagues in the accounting and finance function.

The largest group of usable HR directors' responses was received from the public limited companies, 36 in total, although this was lower than the number of accounting and finance returns. Ten public limited companies declined to participate (including six who returned accounting and finance questionnaires). Once again both the universities and the charities were comparatively willing participants. In the case of the local authorities, 28 of 116 responded (24.1%). The primary care trusts were even more cooperative, 16 of 58 offering responses (27.6%). The least responsive were the government agencies and the professional accounting firms, returning one each, which in the case of the latter organisation had been returned using an accounting and finance questionnaire. Finally, there were 13 unidentifiable responses, all usable, for the HR directors, compared with four in the case of the accounting and finance directors.

Workforce health

The response of the HR directors to the question on the importance accorded to physical health within their organisations, is set out in Table 6.1.

Table 6.1 Importance accorded to physical health

Importance accorded to physical health	Private sector organisations		Public sector and charitable organisations		Unidentifiable organisations		Total	
	N	%	N	%	N	%	N	%
A vital consideration	15	32.6	34	45.3	3	23.1	52	38.8
Very important	22	47.8	28	37.3	8	61.5	58	43.3
Important	7	15.2	13	17.4	2	15.4	22	16.5
A minor consideration	1	2.2	-	-	-	-	1	0.7
Not important at all	1	2.2	-	-	-	-	1	0.7
Total	46	100.0	75	100.0	13	100.0	134	100.0

In excess of 80% of HR directors reported that physical health is regarded as a vital or very important issue within their organisations, with 52 identifying it as a vital consideration at this time. Although there was only a marginal difference between the two principal sub samples, in the case of the public sector and charitable organisations there was greater evidence that physical health was a vital consideration. Overall, however, a chi-square test of independence suggests that there is no association between the type of organisation and the importance accorded to physical health within this sample at the 0.05 level of significance (test statistic: 7.85; df 8).

The pattern of responses to question three on mental health was very similar (Table 6.2).

Table 6.2   Importance accorded to mental health

Importance accorded to mental health	Private sector organisations		Public sector and charitable organisations		Unidentifiable organisations		Total	
	N	%	N	%	N	%	N	%
A vital consideration	14	30.4	37	49.3	4	30.8	55	41.0
Very important	20	43.5	27	36.0	8	61.5	55	41.0
Important	10	21.8	10	13.3	1	7.7	21	15.7
A minor consideration	2	4.3	1	1.4	-	-	3	2.3
Not important at all	-	-	-	-	-	-	-	-
Total	46	100.0	75	100.0	13	100.0	134	100.0

Once again, a little over 80% responded that mental health is regarded as at least a very important issue in their organisations, with the public sector and charitable organisations more skewed towards viewing it as a vital consideration. In this instance, no respondents reported that mental health was considered to be of no importance, although somewhat surprisingly, three (as opposed to one) respondents claimed it to be of only minor importance. The appropriate test statistic was 8.06, again suggesting no association between these variables at the 0.05 level of significance (df 8).

Comments amplifying their responses to questions two and three were scarce in the case of the private sector organisations. A respondent from one of the public limited companies identified the objectives of:

[P]revent[ing] *all work-related physical health problems by means of risk assessment, ergonomic job design and training......and work-related mental health problems by means of structured organisation communication, reporting, appraisal, PDP, time management and assertiveness training.*

Two respondents identified the existence of wellbeing programmes, one adding in relation to question three that the programme includes mental health and stress management, a second that the programme incorporates a 'coping with pressure' initiative. A further public limited company respondent reported that while both physical and mental health are currently viewed as important issues, his aim was that they became recognised as vital considerations.

The public sector and charitable organisation respondents were a little more expansive. Two primary care trust respondents made the link between this particular type of organisation and promoting the health of its own workforce:

Public health is a significant part of our agenda - this starts with our employees.

We are a healthcare organisation. All appointments are health screened prior to an offer of employment being made.

Similar sentiments were present in a charitable organisation:

As a heart charity the organisation believes in acting as a role model. We fund research into health in other organisations and have a similar project starting internally.

Commenting on only reporting 'important' in answer to questions two and three, a local government respondent added:

Whilst within HR the view is very important, the buy-in from team leaders and the rest of the organisation to address and build up [both] *physical and mental health awareness is lower, hence the reduced score.*

Finally, in one of the unidentifiable organisations, the respondent commented:

We have invested in an independent advice and counselling service for all employees, which includes alcohol and drug advice and support.

Question four was designed to elicit information on the existence of arrangements currently in place to monitor workforce health. Table 6.3 indicates that once again in excess of 80% of respondents reported that at least a moderate level of monitoring is currently pursued. Only four respondents reported no such arrangements, two of whom were in the unidentifiable organisations' group, which also reported a marginally higher level of extensive arrangements.

Table 6.3   Provision for monitoring workforce health

Provision for monitoring workforce health	Private sector organisations		Public sector and charitable organisations		Unidentifiable organisations		Total	
	N	%	N	%	N	%	N	%
Extensive	14	30.4	25	33.3	5	38.5	44	32.8
Moderate	25	54.4	39	52.0	5	38.5	69	51.5
Rudimentary	6	13.0	10	13.4	1	7.7	17	12.7
None	1	2.2	1	1.3	2	15.3	4	3.0
Total	46	100.0	75	100.0	13	100.0	134	100.0

The chi-square test of independence once again suggests no association between the variables at the usual level of significance (test statistic: 8.48; df 6).

The majority of respondents elected to offer further information on extant arrangements, belying the overall belief that these are only moderate in extent. Sickness and absence monitoring are extensive, combined with return to work interviews and referrals to occupational health departments. These appeared to be pursued on a formal basis in most occasions, with the relevant information being reported in various forums. Pre-employment health checks were reported as being commonplace together with regular health screening. Mention was also made of Employee Assistance Programmes (EAP), some of which were provided by third parties. Senior staff was sometimes identified as having BUPA as part of their employment package, with colleagues able to access free health checks.

In some instances it was clear that monitoring was comprehensive, as in the comments on the 'moderate' provision reported by two private company respondents:

Primarily through absence recording and monitoring, summary reports from our Employee Assistance supplier, occupational health reports, senior management medical screening, pre-employment medicals and health and safety reports and audits. In addition, extensive planning conducted to address potential issues arising from a pandemic.

Absence monitoring; follow up on long term absence; review of statistics on use of healthcare scheme - by employment category, location, type of illness. Review of use of Employment Assistance Programme - by employment category and nature of underlying cause for usage of the EAP.

A respondent from one of the universities was similarly expansive:

Key reporting arrangements: sickness monitoring trigger part reports. [These are] forwarded to heads of service, rigorous medical referral for long term sick i.e. over three weeks absence, aims to continuously improve sickness levels plus introduction of Active Workforce Co-ordinator, arranging employee-only fitness sessions and health screening, medical; health screening - this is voluntary plus provision of OH service.

A second university respondent identified a wider range of provisions:

Recently published a new stress awareness policy. Have commenced stress awareness training for all managers. Improving our occupational health service. Have a disability advisor. Extensive tools in place for bullying and harassment issues.

The following response from a public limited company suggests that its senior management were beginning to take the challenge of promoting the health and wellbeing of their employees very seriously:

We are currently piloting a trial scheme for one department identified as being at risk of suffering stress. This entails a medical provider carrying out annual physical examinations which include heart and lungs, BMI, blood and urine, sensory, diet, and separate tests for men and women for prostate checks, breast checks and optional mammogram.

Overall, there was no obvious distinction between the two principal sub samples, both of which conveyed the impression of arguably better than moderate monitoring arrangements being in place.

In the light of these responses, it is not too surprising to find that 73.9% of respondents claimed that their organisations had taken some steps to improve the health of their workforces. Table 6.4 illustrates that there is a measure of difference between such provisions in the case of the public sector and charitable organisations and those in the private sector. The chi-square test results do not confirm this, however, demonstrating that there is no apparent association at the 0.05 significance level between the type of organisation and extant initiatives (test statistic: 3.08; df 4).

Table 6.4   Steps taken to improve workforce health

Steps taken to improve workforce health	Private sector organisations		Public sector and charitable organisations		Unidentifiable organisations		Total	
	N	%	N	%	N	%	N	%
Some	32	69.6	58	77.3	9	69.2	99	73.9
Few	10	21.7	14	18.7	2	15.4	26	19.4
None	4	8.7	3	4.0	2	15.4	9	6.7
Total	46	100.0	75	100.0	13	100.0	134	100.0

When the 'few steps' responses are combined with 'some steps' responses, only three of the 75 public sector and charitable organisations' respondents claimed that no such steps had been taken. For the first time, the latter organisations clearly appear to be in the vanguard of thinking about workforce health issues.

As was the case with the accounting and finance directors, a wide range of initiatives was reported by respondents. In the case of the public sector and charitable organisations the most commonly identified activities were associated with helping employees to stop smoking, whether by providing counselling, support groups or a smoke-free environment. Many of these initiatives were identified as long-standing. By comparison dealing with 'stress' was a more recent intervention, although probably on the same scale at the moment, suggesting that it will soon overtake the smoking challenge. Health education, whether in general or in the specific work-life balance sense, was also mentioned by many respondents, with some evidence of an increased number of 'health days' or 'health weeks'. There was less evidence of promoting physical exercise. Several respondents commented on the provision of gymnasium facilities, both in-house and externally (some subsidised). A couple of people identified organised walking groups and one respondent made reference to a policy of encouraging employees to take part in a London to Brighton bike ride event. Similarly, there seemed to be less emphasis on promoting healthy eating, with only a single respondent commenting on the introduction of healthy meals in the dining room. On this evidence, workforce problems with alcohol or drugs were not widespread.

There were one or two outliers reported. In a local authority, as well as a physiotherapy service and access to a chiropractitioner, employees could also undergo acupuncture. A primary care trust viewed its zero tolerance policy to abuse to staff as part of its portfolio of health improvement initiatives, alongside risk assessments, flexible working arrangements and lone working guidance. Several Scottish local authorities were involved in the Scottish Health at Work (SHAW) programme, one currently holding a prestigious gold award. Elsewhere a 'Cultural Officer' had been appointed to lead a number of healthy living activities within a local authority. Finally, another local authority respondent identified the introduction of a successful 'Dawn Day' policy, which allowed employees to register for a day's holiday at short notice rather than a traditional sick day.

In the case of the private sector organisations the range was a little more modest, with the provision of some form of health/illness insurance provision, sometimes free or discounted, and sometimes voluntary, being the most common provision. Wellbeing programmes were the next most popular intervention, followed by regular health screening programmes. Stress monitoring was not accorded the same recognition, although interestingly one respondent in a public limited company referred explicitly to the existence of a 'mental wellbeing' initiative. Only a few respondents cited exercise programmes or access to gymnasium/ leisure club memberships. Smoking cessation initiatives were identified less frequently by HR directors. The only mention of alcohol or drug problems was made by a respondent from one of the unidentifiable organisations. Healthy eating education was also pursued in some organisations, in one case complemented by the recent availability of decaffeinated coffee and tea in the canteen and 'filtered spring water' in all departments.

One or two interesting developments were reported, for instance in one of the public limited companies:

> *We operate on an international scale, with an HIV/AIDS programme - the world's largest private sector initiative. We also focus on reducing exposures to industrial hygiene hazards, providing a lot of employee training for this.*

Reflexology and massage services were identified by a second public limited company respondent, while a second pursued risk assessments for pregnant women, as well as free sight tests and subsidised ophthalmic services, presumably for all employees. At the other end of the spectrum, another public limited company respondent announced that:

On site nurse visits periodically.

It should be recalled, however, that four members of this sub sample, plus a further two in the unidentifiable organisations, whose responses were much closer to those from the private sector organisations, reported that no such steps had been taken by their employers.

The extent of workforce health measurement claimed by this sample was much higher than among accounting and finance directors. Table 6.5 indicates that across the sample as a whole, 56% of organisations are attempting to measure workforce health in some way, with the private sector organisations only very marginally ahead of the rest. This finding is borne out by the relevant test statistic (0.65, df 2).

Table 6.5   Measurement of workforce health

Measurement of workforce health	Private sector organisations		Public sector and charitable organisations		Unidentifiable organisations		Total	
	N	%	N	%	N	%	N	%
Yes	27	58.7	42	56.0	6	46.2	75	56.0
No	19	41.3	33	44.0	7	53.8	59	44.0
Total	46	100.0	75	100.0	13	100.0	134	100.0

To a large extent such measurement took the form of sickness or absence monitoring and the results of health screening initiatives. In some instances measurement was more comprehensive, as in the case of one of the public limited companies operating in the engineering industry:

We have global metrics for occupational ill health, ratified by our OH practitioners. These may be with or without lost time. Our parameters are: musculo-skeletal; respiratory disease; dermatitis; vibration white finger; and various others.

A second public limited company respondent identified:

Statistical annual reports following screening. Also through health surveillance. VDU eyesight screening is carried out. There is lung function screening with the results processed through the Occupational Health Department.

In one of the charities, attempts to extend the measurement process were currently underway:

We are attempting to improve data accuracy in support of provisions [listed previously]. *Then we will begin to compare sickness absence with accidents, EAP reports and OH data. In this way our existing Workforce Annual Status Report will be able to identify specific concerns and point to possible solutions.*

In two of the primary care trusts reference was made to the use of Bradford (Index) scores, an established model for identifying the differential impact of short term absence patterns, while a respondent from one of the universities reported that the institution surveyed the extent of bullying and harassment within the workplace. The most progressive initiative was reported by one of the local authorities, combining the answers to questions five and six:

A 'working well' project has been developed by the Healthy Workplace Manager. This looks at physical activity, healthy eating, stopping smoking and healthy working including back pain, stress management and musculo-skeletal problems. Baseline physical activity has now been measured and we have set a target to increase the level by 9% by June 2009.

At this time, however, such initiatives remain the exception.

Turning to the complementary practice of reporting information on workforce health, it is the public sector organisations that are now in the vanguard, the charitable organisations exhibiting a similar profile as the private sector organisations. Overall, there would appear to be no association between the variables at the 0.05 significance level (test statistic: 1.26; df 2).

Table 6.6   Reporting on workforce health

Reporting on workforce health	Private sector organisations		Public sector and charitable organisations		Unidentifiable organisations		Total	
	N	%	N	%	N	%	N	%
Yes	26	56.5	50	66.7	8	61.5	84	62.7
No	20	43.5	25	33.3	5	38.5	50	37.3
Total	46	100.0	75	100.0	13	100.0	134	100.0

In the great majority of cases, reporting in public sector organisations is restricted to internal reporting. In one of the local authorities such information was reported to Audit Scotland, while a second authority included some workforce health information in its 'Public Performance Report'. Some primary care trust reported externally *e.g.* to the Department of Health, the Scottish Executive or to Strategic Health Authorities. For the rest, the main recipients of workforce health information were middle managers, who received this for their own departments on an on-going basis, or directors and chief executives who were provided with more comprehensive information, albeit less frequently. Local authority respondents also identified providing information to councillors as a group or the relevant council committee with the same frequency. The following systematic reporting arrangements reported by another local authority are clearly untypical:

1. the Corporate Management Team (the 'Board')
2. the Employee Consultative Committee
3. the Personnel Sub-Committee
4. the Cabinet
5. the full Council

As Table 6.6 shows, 56.5% of private sector organisation respondents indicated that their organisations reported information on workforce health. There was less evidence of providing information to middle managers in these organisations, although as it is commonly reported to HR directors (or some equivalent person), they will probably receive it indirectly. HR generally passes the information to the Board. There were also some interesting insights is respect of reporting on workforce health outside of the organisation. Several respondents identified their corporate social responsibility report as a mechanism for reporting such information externally, one directing the research team to its 'Report to Society' that can be accessed on its website. Another respondent commented that some information of this sort was included within the company's governance disclosures within the annual report. Finally, one of the unidentifiable organisation respondents noted that the organisation made this sort of information available in briefings to City analysts.

In the case of the accounting and finance directors, there is evidence that developments in respect of workforce health had reached a plateau, with only limited indication that workforce health is likely to become a more important consideration within the organisation in the future. HR directors were more positive about the future, as is evident from Table 6.7. And while at the 0.05 significance level this is no evident association level between types of organisation and espoused concern, at the next level, 0.10, this is overturned (test statistic: 5.28; df 2).

Table 6.7   Increased concern with workforce health in the future

Increased concern with workforce health in the future	Private sector organisations		Public sector and charitable organisations		Unidentifiable organisations		Total	
	N	%	N	%	N	%	N	%
Yes	25	54.3	48	64.0	4	30.8	77	57.5
No	21	45.7	27	36.0	9	69.2	57	42.5
Total	46	100.0	75	100.0	13	100.0	134	100.0

A number of respondents answered 'no' to this question but again added that this was because it is already of substantial importance. If these responses are factored in, around 60% of the sample was positive about the future, again more particularly in the case of the public sector and charitable organisations. The local authorities are generally in the vanguard, some respondents identifying a lengthy list of initiatives:

The council is introducing a health and wellbeing strategy that is to be fully embedded in the culture of the organisation. There is to be a review of our sickness absence management and the new occupational health contract will provide employee health checks. We are also looking at occupational stress more pro-actively with emphasis on prevention and early intervention.

Introduction of domestic violence guidance for managers and employees. Nurse-led absence reporting pilot study. Monthly workforce sickness statistical analysis. Stress risk assessments. Occupational Health statistical analysis of employee referrals to that service.

In other cases something more adventurous and more formal was being envisaged:

We are soon hoping to provide yoga, pilates, massage and reflexology on-site

More work planned on stress management and we have signed up to HSE's 'Fit3' campaign.

Several of the universities identified stress oriented developments such as improved stress management, stress audits and work-life balance projects. Stress awareness and the promotion of family-friendly working practices were identified by respondents from charitable organisations, while one of the respondents in a primary care trust identified the different issues that confronted such organisations:

Zero tolerance policies concerning the abuse of staff. Risk assessments. Health and safety training for manual handling, fire safety. Improved staff induction procedures.

Many of the same proposals were also highlighted by respondents from the public limited companies and the private companies:

The promotion of 'stress related' illness awareness for managers. Considering introducing an Employee Assistance Programme and extending the existing private medical health facility. Promotion of wellbeing/life balance via a flexible benefits system.

We are continuing to promote the gym, away days with health in mind, offering 'cycle to work' schemes. The company went carbon neutral this year doing much promotion of a healthier environment, both at work and at leisure.

Consideration is being given to training to address preventative illness types prevalent in healthcare statistics. We are also looking at extending EAP provisions to all employees and their dependent families and extended employment medical provision is currently under review.

Intellectual capital

The responses to the initial question in this section of the questionnaire indicate that marginally over 60% are either familiar or very familiar with the terms 'intellectual capital' or 'intangibles', which is much lower than among accounting and finance directors (84%). Consistent with this is the finding that a quarter of respondents are unfamiliar with these terms. Table 6.8 shows that the responses between the private sector and public sector and charitable organisations are very similar. This is reflected in a chi-square statistic of 1.99 (df 6).

Table 6.8   Familiarity with the terms 'intellectual capital' or 'intangibles'

Familiarity with the terms 'intellectual capital' or 'intangibles'	Private sector organisations		Public sector and charitable organisations		Unidentifiable organisations		Total	
	N	%	N	%	N	%	N	%
Very familiar	10	21.7	14	18.7	3	23.1	27	20.1
Familiar	19	41.3	34	45.3	4	30.8	57	42.5
Have heard of them	6	13.0	9	12.0	1	7.7	16	11.9
Unfamiliar	11	24.0	18	24.0	5	38.4	34	25.5
Total	46	100.0	75	100.0	13	100.0	134	100.0

A sizeable number of respondents provided details of their understanding of these two terms. As the following examples, drawn from across the sub sample suggest, they are perceived to relate closely to 'people':

Intellectual capital refers to the psychological contract with employees, capturing their 'discretionary' effort and generally seeking to shape culture through talent management and other approaches that are not 'task/role' based.

Another term is knowledge management. It is directly linked to what people know and how what they know can be utilised to support business and organisational objectives.

Intellectual capital is like the Human Capital within an organisation. As such, effective ways of developing, protecting and managing it are required.

Working in a university, it is well understood that much of the organisation's value is the knowledge, academic standing and research ability of individuals. I would describe this as intellectual capital.

a) *professional/technical know-how of the organisation as enshrined in certain categories of staff; and*

b) *the human capital side of an organisation: the living response to the customer and market environment that gives an organisation the capability to adapt to market changes/new markets and environmental conditions.*

The former refers to the value, skills and experience of the workforce. As an intangible, it is hard to cost the benefit or loss. Through change management methodology one can see the importance given to retaining competence, and one can also see the negative impacts when they are lost.

The last response identifies the difficulties associated with accounting for (valuing) intellectual capital, an issue that was also raised by other respondents:

Intangibles are things like brand, reputation, knowledge and people, which go to make up the value of an organisation, (along with financial capital, assets, equipment, etc.). Intellectual capital is one of those intangibles, although it is very difficult to measure the value of it.

Intellectual capital is a notional value assigned to the 'knowledge bank' represented by the workforce. Intangibles are items which cannot easily be quantified or measured.

A public limited company respondent provided the following sophisticated 'definition':

The knowledge, experience, skills embodied in the workforce. This would include issues across a spectrum from patents or patentable ideas, particular corporate expertise to 'institutional memory'.

At the other end of the spectrum is the observation of a primary care trust respondent:

What I think of - is mine.

Question 11 was concerned with any familiarity respondents had with developments designed to account for intellectual capital, including the Balanced Scorecard or Intellectual Capital Statements. Of the 126 respondents who answered this question, only 13 (10.2%) indicated that they are very familiar with such developments. The private sector organisations sub-sample were the most familiar but only in six of 44 cases (13.6%). If the eight respondents who did not answer this question are taken as being unaware of any developments, in total marginally over half the sample were unaware. By far the most frequently mentioned development was the Balanced Scorecard, although by no means can it be designated a universally familiar reporting framework. A few respondents made reference to the (proposed) Operating and Financial Review, as well as to the EFQM Model of Business Excellence. Investors in People (IIP) was also mentioned together with the 'business dashboard'. A respondent from one of the charities commented that:

We do not talk about our people in these terms

...whilst a 'sceptical' public limited company respondent opined:

Balanced Scorecards seem to take expert judgement and turn it into numbers for no particular reason.

The final question (13) in this section asked how important it is to incorporate intellectual capital within financial statements. A significant number of respondents, 38 (28.4%), declined to answer this particular question, many of them commenting that they simply did not know the answer to this question as it is not one that had previously occurred to them. Of those who did offer a view, 46.9% believed that it was quite important to do so, followed by 20.8% who believed it was very important. Only four respondents took the view that such an action was a distraction, confirming a very different view on this issue when compared with the responses from the accounting and finance directors' sample. One quarter of the private sector organisations' respondents believed this was a very important issue, with 36.4% taking the view it was quite an important issue. In the case of the public sector and charitable organisations the responses were 22.2% and 50% respectively.

The comments offered in association with this question were limited, although some were quite instructive. A respondent from one of the private companies asserted that:

Firstly it starts to place the significance of effective people management/utilisation within the context of financial performance. Secondly the full potential of an organisation can be viewed from a different angle.

Another respondent from a public limited company was not so sure about this:

It depends - you can quantify human capital but it does not really add value to your business. The qualitative is sometimes more important in driving business change.

A university-based respondent posed the following, intriguing question:

Is the RAE [Research Assessment Exercise] *not really a measure of intellectual capital?*

Finally, a second public limited company respondent made a connection with the research project itself:

If this was in place it would sell the business case for investing in health more effectively.

Organisational assets

The responses to the first question in the final section of the HR directors' questionnaire indicate that almost three quarters (73.9%) took the view that workforce health is an organisational asset. Respondents from the public sector and charitable organisations were a little more positive, with those from the private sector slightly less so. Most respondents elected not to provide much in the way of reasoning in support of their answers, whether positive or negative. There was the occasional positive acknowledgement of the importance of the workforce and its health:

> *The intellectual* [workforce] *(R&D and management) is vital for the operation, evolution and sustainability of the company and* [the] *manual* [workforce] *for the production and manufacture of products. Health, both physical and mental, is vital for both.*

> *It should be - since the growth and development of the organisation is directly related to the wellbeing, growth and development of its employees.*

> *The business is people driven - they are our only asset.*

In one or two cases there was evidence of a more qualified support, as in the case of one of the private companies:

> *Healthy employees are more effective people. Absenteeism is lowered. Job performance is enhanced. Productivity is enhanced. Morale is enhanced because the company cares. There are less insurance and liability claims.*

The following pair of responses, one from the private sector, the other from the public sector, indulged in a little reflection on what the term 'asset' encapsulates in this context:

Health of employees is important and employers have a duty to ensure this is not unreasonably put at risk - but I cannot see 'health' as an asset and only a liability if it was very far below the norm or poor as a result of organisational negligence leading to financial loss.

Yes, but it depends on the definition of 'organisational asset'. Staff are our biggest and most important asset so their health has to be linked as part of that 'asset'.

Two local authority respondents and one from a charitable organisation were clearly not persuaded by such a view:

Cannot put it on the balance sheet.

It cannot be quantified in any meaningful way.

The view of a charitable organisation respondent was unequivocal about advancing such a view:

Health belongs to the individual not the organisation.

While a second respondent from this sector simply opined:

This is a bit sophisticated for us at present.

Ten of the 134 respondents declined to provide an answer to question 16, which asked whether it is possible to put a financial value on workforce health. Of those who provided an answer, 63.7% took the view that it was possible with 31.5% taking the opposite view. Six respondents indicated that they were uncertain whether or not this was possible, a response that was added by themselves. There was a sizeable difference between the private sector organisation and the public sector and charitable organisation sub sample responses, however. In the case of the former, 54.8% took a positive view, compared with 69.6% in the case of the latter. Closer analysis indicates that there is a very high level of support for this proposition in the case of the 16 primary care trusts (81%), although among the charitable organisations there was a lower level of support than among the generality of private sector organisations (9 of 21).

It therefore seems apposite to begin by considering the reasons provided for answering affirmatively with some from the primary care trusts. The following are largely representative of the general view:

> *If employees are unhealthy then you are likely to see a decrease in performance which would reduce profit. Also cost is sickness absence and managing the process, occupational health referrals and phased work returns.*

> *Healthier workforce, higher productivity levels plus greater social* [and] *economic benefits in communities. Healthier communities less financial impact on the NHS.*

Respondents appear to be identifying cost with financial value, particularly the cost of absence due to sickness and ill health. A third primary care trust respondent identified using the Bradford Index to quantify a 'Bradford score' in combination with the 'cost of agency staff'. Similar views were expressed by respondents from the public sector, including a local authority employee:

If there is poor workforce health and an increase in sickness absence levels, costs will rise as measures are implemented to cover the staff absences.

Not everybody was convinced, including this pair of respondents from a local authority and a charitable organisation respectively:

The benefits of maintaining and improving the health and wellbeing of employees are not quantifiable.

Don't know how you would put a definite figure on something so intangible.

Finally, sitting somewhere in between were several respondents who were not as yet entirely convinced.

Probably but don't know how. Would be notional.

In theory but extremely complex. Is an Oxford geographer worth two Heriot-Watt accountants?

Have yet to see simple practical examples.

Unfortunately, the majority of respondents from private sector organisations did not offer much elaboration on why they took a negative view on placing a financial value on workforce health. One private company respondent sought to differentiate between 'cost' and 'value' approaches:

It is possible to give an accurate estimate of costs around certain health effects: sickness absence; turnover and recruitment; pensions for ill health; claims, but not some of the intangibles around wellbeing leading to increased productivity.

A colleague from a public limited company articulated the difficulty very concisely:

You cannot quantify the value of health intervention.

Others were less negative in their assessment:

Again in theory yes. Logic would suggest that if we can measure the cost of employee ill-health, through lost working days, etc, we could put a value on employee 'good health'.

Some were positively upbeat about the situation, including a water industry respondent:

The representative cost of a case of work-related ill health (resulting in absence) in the water industry has been calculated and verified and approved by the HSE chair.

In due course, the research team was able to discuss this cost model with the respondent, details of which are reported in the next chapter.

Question 17 in the HR directors' questionnaire, which corresponds to question 22 in the accounting and finance directors' questionnaire, asks how respondents think information on workforce health could best be provided to users. Eight possible options were provided for respondents, as shown in Table 6.9.

Table 6.9   Means of reporting on workforce health to users

Means of reporting on workforce health to users	Private sector organisations		Public sector and charitable organisations		Unidentifiable organisations		Total	
	N	%	N	%	N	%	N	%
1. As financial data in financial statements	5	10.9	8	10.7	-	-	13	9.7
2. As non-financial data in financial statements	4	8.7	5	6.7	4	30.8	13	9.7
3. As a combination of 1 and 2	18	39.1	39	52.0	4	30.8	61	45.5
4. As financial data supplementary to financial statements	3	6.5	4	5.3	-	-	7	5.2
5. As non-financial data supplementary to financial statements	4	8.7	2	2.6	3	23.0	9	6.7
6. As some combination of 4 and 5	5	10.9	9	12.0	-	-	14	10.4
7. Other	3	6.5	3	4.0	1	7.7	7	5.2
8. None of these	4	8.7	5	6.7	1	7.7	10	7.6
Total	46	100.0	75	100.0	13	100.0	134	100.0

The chi-square test statistic for this table is 20.21, which with 14 degrees of freedom suggests that at the 0.05 level, there appears to be no association between the type of organisation and preferred mode of reporting workforce health to users.

By a considerable margin combining financial data, such as key performance indicators, with a non-financial narrative within the financial statements (option three) was the most favoured option. In the case of the public sector and charitable organizations over half of the respondents (52%) chose this option, compared with a little under 40% of private sector organisation respondents. A primary care trust respondent explained this choice in the following terms:

Enables the organisation and its senior managers to have an accurate understanding of how poor health of its workforce can impact on performance so needs to be in both qualitative and quantitative data - shows both the financial and moral requirements. An organisation has to look after the health and wellbeing of its workforce.

Similar sentiments were expressed by a pair of respondents from local government and one from a public limited company:

KPIs just give the overview and do not provide reasons for why the financial data may be as it is. Combination of both provides more detail and gives reasoning for the figure.

It is necessary to illustrate trends and patterns or potential causes of absence to highlight the risks to the organisation and what action needs to be in place to manage these short and long term. Figures alone do not provide a complete picture.

It may be possible to put this into financial figures but it is also good to have an informative narrative to explain how the figures were arrived at.

The powerful appeal of a combination of numbers and narratives is affirmed by the finding that option six, combining these in a supplementary statement, was the second most favoured option.

Using either financial information or non-financial information within financial statements was viewed as preferable to the alternative of the same within some supplementary statement. Further elaboration was uncommon, however, although the following responses from a university and a charity suggest that traditional conceptions of accounting continue to hold sway in some quarters:

I feel intellectual capital is of equal importance as tangible assets. Research leaders bring a significant contribution in terms of innovation.

To be taken seriously at Board level, it needs to have a demonstrable cost.

Seven respondents took the view that an alternative approach to providing such information was desirable. For two local authority respondents:

Workforce health should be reported separately to the appropriate committees e.g. Corporate Health and Safety, Employee Joint Consultative Committee, outlining the current state of workforce health, improvements, areas for improvement, and this should include financial statements.

Must be stand-alone to achieve a high profile. A total record of illness frequency with cases to be investigated and learning achieved

This view was shared by a respondent from a public limited company:

Health merits its own separate report. It overlaps with CSR and H and S agendas in an organisation. HSE and the government are already driving the reporting of health in company annual reports.

A second public limited company respondent rejected a financial approach:

I do not believe the bureaucracy involved in tabulating financial data would be worth the effort. Far better to focus on systems and prevention/detection of health issues. A consistent approach to valuation would be difficult - as each business has different processes and cost bases.

Not everybody was convinced, however, including the respondent from one of the private companies who took the view that:

I can see no reason why such information should be provided.

In the case of the accounting and finance directors' survey only one respondent reported any awareness of initiatives elsewhere to account for workforce health. Despite the low overall response rate to this question (73.1%), the position within this sample was significantly better, 21 responding affirmatively. Nine were from the private sector organisations, the remainder from public and charitable organisations. There were no respondents from the unidentifiable group who answered 'yes' to this question. For the most part detail was sketchy but a couple of people mentioned the Chartered Institute for Personnel and Development and the Institute of Health and Productivity Management. A public limited company respondent identified Nestle as having 'a very good business case established'. Only a minority of respondents identified some level of awareness with multiple projects:

Scotland's Health at Work (SHAW) initiative. Government's Health, Work and Wellbeing Strategy. FIT 3(HSE).

Emergency Capacity Building Project. Interagency project. People in Aid, London. Stress in Humanitarian Workers. SPERE project. UN project.

EU Safety and Health Agency. The ILO. DuPont (in USA).

Two further respondents, both from public sector and charitable organisations also acknowledged multiple projects, adding 'Too many to mention'.

Finally, respondents were asked to add further comments if they wished. Only a very small minority of respondents chose to do so, including the following supportive comment from a public limited company respondent:

> *I am pleased to be of any assistance and happy to see that the business case for Occupational Health is not as big a sell or struggle as it used to be.*

Two respondents had issues with the questionnaire itself:

> *Interested to learn why 'workforce health' is being defined narrowly e.g. physical or mental health rather than taking a more holistic view of both organisational health and individual wellbeing.*

> *I'm not sure that vague questions such as these will add very much to knowledge in this area.*

A fourth respondent took the opportunity to question the added value of accounting for workforce health:

> *As a not-for-profit organisation, I would be concerned about the costs of collecting and managing the data.*

A more subtle critique of such exercises was advanced by a local authority respondent.

Local government suffers from 'paralysis by analysis', so efforts to achieve Best Value targets often mask real problems. This County Council seems more concerned with getting to a Best Value target of c7 days (laudable from a staff health perspective!) than analysing problem areas - not the least of which is the cost involved.

Summary

The responses from the HR directors indicate that they believe the health of their workforces is regarded as being of significant importance in their various organisations. Their responses on mental health were evenly distributed between the vital and very important categories, both at 41%, while in the case of physical health, marginally more responded it was of importance than a vital consideration. In both instances the public sector and charitable organisations' respondents were more inclined to view these as issues of being a vital consideration. Almost a third of respondents believed that extensive arrangements were presently in place to monitor workforce health, while 52% felt them to moderate, a more positive perspective.

The principal monitoring mechanism was again some form of sickness or absence recording system, followed by Occupational Health provisions. Reference to Employee Assistance Programmes was more common within this sample who also identified the greater use of surveys, particularly in relation to stress at work, among employees. The promotion of workforce health was reported to be actively in place by 74% of respondents. Those in the public sector and charitable organisations reported marginally higher levels of activity than their private sector counterparts, although the range of initiatives identified was largely the same across both sub samples, with no particular initiative being very widely pursued.

In terms of measuring and reporting workforce health, 56% of respondents indicated that there was some measurement activity in place, with sickness or absence recording by far the most common example. Reporting was claimed by 63% of respondents, mainly of the latter information, to senior management within enterprises and in the case of public sector and charitable organisations, also to a range of regulatory agencies.

In response to the final question in this section of the questionnaire, well in excess of half the respondents took the view that plans are in place to make workforce health a more important consideration in their organisations in the future. This is very much greater than the levels reported by accounting and finance directors, confirming that overall those HR directors who responded to the questionnaire were generally more positive about issues relating to workforce health within their organisations. As in the case of the accounting and finance directors, the public sector and charitable organisations respondents were again more favourably disposed than their colleagues in the private sector organisations.

Fewer than two thirds of respondents claimed to be either familiar or very familiar with the term intellectual capital. The majority identified it with human capital, while a sizeable number also linked intellectual capital with knowledge management. Nevertheless, 57% of respondents were at least familiar with how it might be possible to account for intellectual capital, almost the same level as for accounting and finance directors; 10% of respondents claimed to be very familiar. The Balanced Scorecard was again the most widely recognised approach to reporting, although alternatives were also identified including the EFQM model, human capital reporting, Investors in People and the 'business dashboard'.

Possibly because relatively few respondents were familiar with the intellectual capital concept, many declined to answer question 13. Of those who did, 21% thought it very important to incorporate intellectual capital within financial statements, 47% thought it quite important and only 3% a distraction. Taken together, these findings indicate that although the concept of intellectual capital may not be as widely understood among HR directors as it is among their accounting and finance director counterparts, those who are familiar with it are reasonably positive about its importance, particularly as it encompasses people. Respondents from the public sector and charitable organisations were slightly more positive once again.

On the issue of whether workforce health qualified as an organisational asset, 74% of those who responded said that it is, a significantly different finding than in the case of accounting and finance directors. Many respondents identified a link with increased productivity or capacity to deliver better services when the workforce is fitter. Fewer (68%) respondents thought that it was possible to place a financial value on workforce health, although a large number of them took the view that this might be a difficult thing to do, some recognising that such a value might only be notional. There was a degree of uncertainty evident in response to the question on how best to report information on workforce health, 46% identifying a combination of financial data such as key performance indicators and a narrative within the financial statements. Relatively little support was evident for using supplementary information, which suggests that HR directors currently regard financial statements as having significant credibility within the upper echelons of management.

The question on existing initiatives to account for workforce health elicited an interesting response, with no fewer than 21 respondents claiming some knowledge. Many of the initiatives identified departed from what their counterparts in accounting and finance might recognise as an 'account'. This suggests that, implicitly at least, HR directors have a more open mind about what accounting for workforce health might encompass. Responses to the invitation to offer further comments covered a number of issues including the cost of such exercises and the rather narrow way in which the questionnaire conceptualised workforce health. On balance, these responses tended to be supportive of the perceived objectives of the project.

7 CASE ORGANISATIONS

Introduction

From the outset, the research team held the view that it would be desirable to provide information on thinking about workforce health as an organisational asset gathered from a small number of organisations that, with justification, could be regarded as being in the vanguard of such developments. Insights gained in the course of interviews with representatives from such organisations would amplify the more positive findings from the questionnaire surveys as well as provide indications of current 'best practice' in the UK. As expected, a number of survey respondents offered invitations to engage in a measure of continued dialogue about the research project. These were duly pursued, resulting in the following three case studies, one in a privatised utilities company operating in southern England, a second in a large Scottish local authority, and in the third case a global pharmaceuticals company. All three organisations were provided with the opportunity to comment on and/or amend the following text, with each also readily agreeing to the use of their names in any subsequent publications.

South West Water

South West Water (SWW) is a subsidiary of the Pennon Group, together with Viridor, which operates in the waste management industry. Both subsidiaries had similar turnovers in 2006-7, although SWW's operating profit was more than three times that of Viridor, at £156.8 million, an increase of 10.8% over the previous year, the bulk of which has been channelled into one of Europe's biggest environmental investment programmes. SWW is the licensed provider of water and sewerage services for Cornwall and Devon, as well as parts of Dorset and Somerset. In total it serves a region of almost 10,300 square kilometres, with 1.65 million residents and around eight million visitors annually. Average daily supply by SWW is 440 million litres of treated water, with accompanying daily disposal of 250 million litres of waste water.

The culture of the water industry has traditionally been characterised by a strong commitment to public service. This has continued since the privatisation of the industry in 1989, in spite of pressures introduced by massive construction and engineering programmes in a commercial context, a continual reduction in the size of the workforce and the increased use of new technology. Nevertheless, for those operatives in the field e.g. manning water and waste water treatment works or engaged in maintaining this vital element of the regional infrastructure, there is considerable evidence of continuing pride in serving their customers. Locally, employment with SWW is viewed as being highly desirable, not only due to the relatively limited range of alternative year round employments in the region but because the company pays well and is generally regarded as a good employer. Throughout the interviews it was continually affirmed that SWW is not untypical of parallel organisations in the UK, and that to some extent this is a consequence of the stance taken by the industry regulator (OFWAT) since privatisation.

SWW was very keen to outline its workforce health provisions for the public record. Health and safety are indisputably viewed as important to the organisation. Although it is not possible to say that the safety aspect is wholly under control, despite a reduction from 143 accidents per 1,000 employed at the time of privatisation to 14 accidents per 1,000 employees in 2002 and again to 11 in 2006, the promotion of increased occupational health would now appear to be recognised as an exercise through which significant value can be added. The three principal health challenges are identified as stress, musculo-skeletal disorders and gastro-enteritis. The latter is an ever present threat to employees in this industry, working as they do with waste water. Stress is increasingly prevalent among both head office staff and staff employed on site, who find themselves working with increasing levels of technology and in some cases in relative isolation. Strenuous efforts have been made over the past decade to educate the SWW workforce about the importance of them sharing responsibility for their own health with management. All of the interviewees, one of whom was a trade union representative, agreed that significant progress had been made in relation to occupational health and that the workforce had embraced this aspect of the prevailing corporate culture. However, there was still much more that could be achieved.

Without question, a major factor in the success evident at SWW is the presence of a Health, Safety and Security Manager wholly committed to the promotion of a preventive health and safety culture. Appointed in 1991, following a long career with the Health and Safety Executive, he has assembled a team he is confident will continue to successfully grow the occupational health and safety culture following his retirement at the end of 2007. To some degree this will be facilitated by his continued promotion of occupational health activities at the industry level, which he has spearheaded since the later 1990s. As is so often the case, SWW's vanguard role is largely attributable to this charismatic individual who has pursued the project with passion. This is widely recognised by colleagues, including the senior trade union representative who twice expressed the view that since his appointment the health and safety situation had improved '5,000 per cent'!

As a member of the UK water industry, SWW directs and is an active participant in the 'Clear Water 2010' (CW2010) initiative, launched in 2000 as part of the Government's 'Securing Health Together' programme. The latter have been informed by the findings of The Frank Davies Project (FDP) report, originally published in April 1998 and produced by SWW on behalf of the Health and Safety Executive and the UK water industry by Rob Gwyther. The strategic objective of the FDP was to 'identify accident and ill health costs in the water industry and promote the commercial case for health and safety management'.

The report identified four types of ill health that it regarded as prevalent in the industry: work related upper limb disorder; hand arm vibration syndrome; occupational stress; and noise induced hearing loss. It estimated that the 'representative cost' of a case of work-related ill health in the industry was £8,650. It also identified the benefits of two prevention programmes underway at SWW, on related upper limb disorder, which was immediately self-financing and on hand arm vibration syndrome, which was expected to become self-financing within two years. In combination these initiatives were estimated to deliver savings in excess of £100,000 per year.

The FDP report provides further details on the cost of work-related ill health, which it defines as an 'evident reduction in the health of an employee confirmed by an Occupational Health professional as being due, or partly due, to working conditions'. Nine elements of cost are identified: employee lost time; investigation time; operational inefficiencies; treatment costs; Occupational Health physician costs; Occupational Health nurse costs; liaison with HSE; claims costs; and settlements. It was information gathered from South West Water and Yorkshire Water about these costs that was used to arrive at the figure of £8,650 identified in the report.

The CW2010 initiative commits the UK water industry to achieving three targets by the end of 2010. The first target is to reduce cases of work-related illness by 20%. Target two is to promote improved rehabilitation and recovery. The final target is a 30% reduction in days lost to work-related illness. Additionally, half of these improvements were to be accomplished by the end of 2004. The mid-term *Clear Vision 2004* report published in Spring 2005 notes that there had been little or no progress in respect of the first target, probably due to a steep rise in reports of work-related ill health in 2002, to some degree the result of an increased focus on it . Progress was evident in the case of musculo-skeletal disorders, despite an increased incidence in 2004. Nevertheless, the report's authors are confident that the initiative will reach this target by 2010. In the case of target two there has been 'little progress' evident, the report's authors believing that 'more could be done' to improve return to work times. Describing target three as 'crucial', the authors report that by the end of 2004 the situation had worsened as compared with 2001 but that a reduction in days lost would be evident by 2010, albeit probably not the 30% target figure. The main difficulty lies with musculo-skeletal disorders; while impressive improvements are confidently expected in the case of both stress and gastro-enteritis, despite the fall in number of cases of musculo-skeletal disorders, the length of associated absences looks likely to translate into no reduction in days lost per 1,000 full-time employees. In order to meet the 30% overall reduction in days lost, the industry must seek even more improvements in the case of stress and gastro-enteritis while continuing to improve the effectiveness of musculo-skeletal disorders interventions.

SWW estimates that the current annual financial cost due to work-related ill health is around £2 million, two thirds of which would seem to be the result of stress. As a principal player in the CW2010 initiative, the organisation has embraced the challenge posed by musculo-skeletal disorders in a robust way. SWW's Manual Handling Revitalisation programme has reduced days lost to such absences by 33.6% during the past two years. The programme combines significant capital investment with ergonomic and engineering expertise, and entails intensive workforce training and commitment. It forms one element of a comprehensive Occupational Health regime that SWW has established during the past decade, a health culture that is strongly embedded across the organisation and widely embraced by all staff.

Within this culture there is a fundamental acceptance that health, like safety, is not a given. It is something that must be constantly worked at by all employees. The emphasis is firmly on prevention, knowing how the organisation can make employees unwell and taking the necessary action to reduce and ultimately minimise such factors. It is now accepted that there is little long term benefit in employees being absent from work, recovering from their organisation induced illness, only to return to their job and risk a recurrence of ill heath, absence and organisational inefficiency. In order to rectify such situations it is necessary to invest the time and resources to bring about the enhanced health environment that workers deserve, and which are now recognised to impact on the long term performance, including financial performance, of the business.

The Occupational Health service that SWW has in place is outsourced to an external provider. A full-time adviser is based at headquarters, in Exeter, although she travels around the region as required in order to promote health and pursue investigations. Referral to Occupational Health is via line managers and restricted to cases where there is believed to be some pattern of causation; the general practitioner system remains the first port of call for general unwellness (although subsequent referrals to Occupational Health do occur). The in-house adviser has access to a wide range of medical and related expertise via her own employers. This provision is widely regarded as a success, a significant improvement on an earlier arrangement that lacked the necessary transparency to make it a success. Although recognised as part of SWW's management structure, the Occupational Health service is greatly valued by all employees and widely subscribed.

The nature of SWW's business results in some obstacles persisting to deny maximum success of the health culture. Around 600 employees are spread across a wide geographical area, some of whom work in isolation for relatively long periods. This results in difficulties for the induction process, at which point the existing health arrangements are outlined to new employees, along with many other relevant items. Of necessity, it is operations managers who play a vital role in this regard and while as a group they are regarded as being highly committed to the existing provision, individual managers can easily, sometimes unintentionally, downplay its significance. Despite the rapid strides made in communication technology in recent years, related technological advances have meant that on-site workers may experience new demands on their (mental) health, which again may go unnoticed by their line managers. Similarly, such a large geographical area poses a problem to the Occupational Health adviser in relation to the capacity to pursue investigation work. While the prevailing health culture is reasonably well financed, budgetary constraints always exist.

Finally, the Health, Safety and Security manager who has done so much to establish, promote and inspire SWW's work health initiative identifies 'presenteeism' as an issue that he wishes to explore. As noted in chapter three, this is a problem that has already attracted the attention of some Scandinavian researchers. At SWW the specific problem is identified as being with those employees who come to work when they are unwell. Again the focus is not on those who have colds, minor stomach upsets, hangovers, etc, rather workers who, for whatever reason, elect to disguise symptoms of work-related ill-health, particularly stress and musculo-skeletal disorders. In his view, the resultant cost of such practices is probably much higher than the £8,650 figure identified in the FDP report, and therefore worth tackling head on. At the time of the interviews a questionnaire that had recently been developed in conjunction with a specialist at the Occupational Health provider was scheduled to be distributed within the organisation. In due course it was hoped that a multiplier could be established that would be used to educate workers about the true costs of their well-intentioned actions.

In summary, SWW can lay claim to having established an exemplary scheme over the past decade, largely as a result of the vision and energy of one individual. He is very confident that his legacy will endure after his imminent 'retirement', a view echoed by a second interviewee. At the moment there is certainly no evidence of complacency, there being a long way to go before ill health has been eradicated at SWW. It seems likely that entrenched practices amongst older employees out in the field, particularly those working alone, will be difficult to dislodge. Putting plasters over cuts and then continuing to work persists. Similarly, there is continued under-reporting of one-day absences due to gastric problems, something the industry has perhaps taken for granted and now inadvertently disguises as a result of providing relatively high remuneration to its employees. A further point of some interest is that during discussions there was little or no mention of the health of headquarters' staff. Obviously they have ready access to the Occupational Health adviser located in Exeter. Beyond this there was reference to attempts to promote healthy eating in the canteen and the availability of local gym membership at a reduced rate, a facility not available to field workers due to logistics. In the light of the significant progress that has been made with their colleagues in the field, further consideration of what can be accomplished here may prove to deliver impressive results.

South Lanarkshire Council

South Lanarkshire Council (SLC) is Scotland's fifth largest local authority, providing services to 306 thousand people with a current budget of £569 million. It covers 1,772 square kilometres, from its northern border with Glasgow, and the urban burghs of Rutherglen and Cambuslang, to Dumfries and Galloway in the south. Overall it is a predominantly rural area, with Hamilton, the site of SLC's headquarters, and East Kilbride, Scotland's first New Town, its largest urban centres, together with the Clydesdale market towns of Lanark and Carluke. Labour currently has the greatest number of councillors on SLC, followed by the Scottish National Party. The provision of high quality education is accorded a major priority by the council, with 42% of budget allocated to the education service. A further 18% is allocated to social work services, indicating that SLC is responsible for the administration of a relatively poor area, as is the case for most of the rest of the West of Scotland.

As an authority, SLC currently employs approximately 16,500 people across seven resource groups and a limited company providing leisure services within its borders. In addition to education and social work there are resource groups covering community, enterprise and housing and technical services, together with the two support functions of finance and information technology and corporate services. The corporate resources group has 242 staff deployed across four areas: administration services; corporate communications and public affairs; legal services; and personnel services, and a central research unit, all within a budget of a little over £16 million. The personnel services web page identifies that safety is a high priority, adding that:

> [C]ouncil employees are encouraged through the council's commitment to Scotland's Health at Work campaign to adopt healthy lifestyles.

It is perhaps worthwhile recalling at this point that the West of Scotland as a whole continues to exhibit some of the lowest levels of life expectancy in both the UK and Europe.

SLC began to take active steps to promote workforce health in 2001. The initiative was driven by the Chief Executive who recognised it to be a key strategic imperative within the authority's pursuit of the highest levels of service delivery, securing extensive cooperation from the trade unions, who have consistently been involved in developing policy. As the name of the initiative 'Maximising Attendance' suggests, initially it was a concern with the high levels of absence evident amongst employees that seems to have triggered action. As reported in chapter three, public sector employees in the UK exhibit relatively high levels of absenteeism. Six years later, SLC still returns absence levels of 8.9 days (3.8%) per employee, acknowledged to be above the CBI national average, but it has seen its own performance improve significantly. This has contributed to SLC's accomplishments towards becoming the best performing council in Scotland, as well as being an 'employer of choice' in the West of Scotland. More significantly, the initial emphasis on reducing absenteeism has evolved into what is regarded as a 'holistic and positive approach to absence, health and wellbeing', which SLC believes is not typical of local authorities, a sphere in which it believes itself to be at the cutting edge of proactive practice. Equally, it is conceded that there are probably larger organisations within Scotland (the Royal Bank of Scotland being cited as an example) who are further along the road in this regard.

SLC's growing concern with absence, health and wellbeing is recognised and promoted as a crucial element of the authority's broader customer-centred service delivery culture. The delivery of services is recognised to be seriously undermined by high levels of absenteeism, which also has the further consequence of taking financial resources away from the process. While not all absenteeism is the result of ill health, any initiative designed to reduce health related absenteeism promises to restore delivery capacity, even after factoring in the observation that any such initiative is never cost free. The corollary of focusing on health rather than absenteeism is to broaden out to consider a much wider set of factors that might impinge upon the employee's capacity for service delivery, hence the earlier identification of a holistic approach to absence, health and wellbeing. Despite being successfully embedded in SLC's employment culture, health promotion is not a feature that is emphasised strongly when recruiting staff. The reasoning is that other features seem to be more attractive to prospective employees, including flexible working, which has its obvious work-life balance or wellbeing implications. So although a concern for workforce health is not regarded as a significant job choice factor, it is something employees soon learn about when they join the authority, which in the main seems to reinforce their satisfaction with their new employment.

The authority has developed a comprehensive approach to promoting the health of employees as an aspect of its wider absence management programme, the main emphasis being placed upon preventive action. New staff are required to undergo pre-employment health checks; night workers are required to undergo annual health assessments; drivers also are required to have regular health and fitness assessments; and hearing checks are performed on those employees regularly subject to excessive noise. The responsibility for ensuring that employees avail themselves of these provisions lies with managers, viewed as a designation that includes chargehands and supervisors, as well as those with the title of manager. These routine services are provided by SLC's Occupational Health service. Managers are also able to refer employees suffering from musculo-skeletal conditions to Occupational Health for treatment in the first instance. The extent of these conditions is such that employees may in turn be referred to an externally contracted physiotherapy service that provides free treatment for employees, with SLC meeting the costs incurred, and employees given time off work to attend the Occupational Health service that also handles those employees who have concerns about their blood pressure or cholesterol levels, as well as such conditions as vibration white finger.

Employees also have access to a wider range of health services. In the case of concerns about stress, managers are required to refer their staff to an Employee Support Officer based within the personnel services function, who is able to provide initial advice on stress management and identify the appropriate intervention including the availability of counselling services. Early intervention is recognised to benefit both the individual employee and the authority, with less time and thus less human resource being lost. In instances where an individual reports absence due to stress, s/he is automatically referred to the Employee Support Officer who then sets in train the same process designed to assist the individual to return to work. In such cases the individual's manager is also contacted and relevant enquiries are pursued. Once again prevention is clearly recognised to be a preferable option to pursue, hence the earlier reference to SLC embracing proactive practices.

The authority has also established an Employee Counselling Service designed to deal with a range of more serious employee problems. Among these is alcohol or drug misuse as well as depression or similar stress related conditions. The same service also deals with financial difficulties or domestic problems, both of which may have a link with medical conditions, together with bereavement. Employees can approach the service directly or indirectly through the offices of their trade union. As a matter of course such individuals are treated in a sympathetic fashion and provided with appropriate support including participation in formal addiction counselling or similar programmes where these are available. At the opposite end of the spectrum, the authority is in the process of exploring the benefits of a range of alternative therapy sessions, offering limited access to employees at a discounted price. These include massage, reflexology, reiki and aromatherapy, all of which are regarded as promoting feelings of relaxation and wellbeing. Finally, SLC has a no smoking policy and has trained a group of counsellors to help those employees who wish to stop smoking.

Complementing the above provisions, and again underpinned by a commitment to preventing ill health, the authority recognises that it must also educate its employees about the benefits of the lifestyle changes they can make that will improve their personal health and reduce their absence from work. In addition to commonplace initiatives on smoking cessation and 'healthy eating' menus in all staff canteens, the authority encourages its staff to cycle to work through a scheme that allows them to purchase a bicycle and pay for it in instalments out of their salary, net of tax. All leisure services provided by SLC are available at a 25% discount. More inventive ways of promoting personal health have also been embraced. Recently the authority has staged a series of plays on men's health issues, following the earlier success of a play on breast cancer. Once again, the trade unions have been fully supportive of these initiatives.

In response to questions on 'presenteeism', it was assuring to learn that such concerns are no longer believed to be commonplace within SLC. While it may previously have been perceived that local authority employment was an 'easy option', in the sense of many jobs making few demands on their incumbents, SLC believes that it has been highly successful in developing a culture in which employees take significant pride in delivering service to their customers. The intrinsic rewards that this brings have largely outweighed dissatisfaction attendant on having to work a little bit harder. This is not to claim that the easy option sub-culture has been totally eradicated in SLC. Pockets of resistance persist despite the emphasis on service delivery and its centrality to the competition that Audit Scotland promotes between local authorities. While the origins of the SLC's concerns with workforce health lay in an instrumental drive to reduce damaging levels of absenteeism, in the interests of enhanced service delivery, there was now a realisation by all parties that it is in no one's interests to come to work ill, whether knowingly or otherwise. Promoting high levels of health awareness among the workforce also encompasses educating employees that there is no reason to come to work if one is unwell. Sanctions will not be applied to genuinely sick employees, beyond those which form part of their contract of employment. This also applies to individuals who are identified as being ill as a result of a health check. Consequently, the advent of absence management places obligations on both employee and employer.

SLC is proud of the progress it has made in respect to its workforce health provision. It was the first local authority in Scotland to be presented with a silver award by Scotland's Health at Work (SHAW), an organisation formed in 1996. The authority is in the process of securing a Healthy Working Lives silver award, an initiative launched in February 2007, and thereafter proposes to proceed to its new gold award. A further measure of the authority's standing in this sphere have been invitations for officers to present at recent HSE 'good practice' seminars. The key to success is that the place of work health promotion is understood as an element of a broader organisational culture that appeals to the great majority of the staff. Although initially a top-down initiative, with potentially damaging roots in an absence management regime, the cooperation of the authority's trade unions and a policy of high transparency have contributed to significant advance. There are, however, some dangers inherent in the existing arrangements. Once absence is reduced to an acceptable level, not least as a result of a concomitant rise in workforce health, there may be a temptation to reduce the size of the workforce in an attempt to divert more funding towards services. In due course this may result in a return of higher levels of absenteeism and ill health, although not in the short term. No less worrying is the crucial role that managerial staff has in making the arrangements work. It is conceded that there is not yet total buy-in among the existing cadre of managers and that on occasion individual managers have to be reminded of their responsibilities. As new managers are appointed it is vital that they are made fully aware of these responsibilities and their contribution to the overall mission of the authority. Finally, such initiatives have the tendency to become increasingly expensive to fund, while incremental gains may reduce. As with all discretionary expenditure, in times of financial stringency the temptation to reduce funding can prevail. However, there is no plan to reduce effort or investment in the 'Maximising Attendance' initiative, the authority and its senior management are constantly seeking innovative and effective ways to encourage employee attendance at work.

AstraZeneca plc

AstraZeneca plc (AZ) was formed in 1999 following the merger of the Swedish pharmaceuticals company Astra with Zeneca, the pharmaceuticals business created when ICI split into two companies in 1993. The company is engaged in the research, development, manufacture/supply, sales/marketing and distribution of prescription medicines. It has a major presence in the following fields of medical need: cancer; cardiovascular; gastrointestinal; infection; neuroscience; and respiratory and inflammatory conditions. AZ's sales in 2007 were $29.6 billion, with a global workforce of approximately 60,000. The company is in the process of a major downsizing exercise in the face of increased pressures within the industry. About half of this workforce is employed in three national 'hubs', the USA, Sweden and the UK. The latter employs in excess of 9,000 people at eight locations. The company's largest UK Research and Development site is at Alderley Park in Cheshire, with further facilities in Loughborough. A large manufacturing plant is located at Macclesfield in Cheshire. The remainder of the company's operations are spread around the globe, including in Europe, Japan, China and India.

As a consequence of the nature of the chemical industry, health and safety had always been major considerations for AZ's UK predecessors ICI, Zeneca, and Astra. A preventive approach to occupational health has been very evident over the years with 'control' and 'containment' practices being increasingly used to prevent physical problems such as dermatitis, occupational asthma and noise-induced hearing loss. Over the last 20-30 years the mental aspects of occupational health have come more into focus particularly driven by a series of changes in the external business environment. By the mid 1990s mental health had become a dominant health concern and a number of initiatives were started. It was recognised that employees are the company's most important resource, and their welfare is essential to maintaining an inventive, productive and profitable organisation. The Chief Financial Officer in 2006 was quoted as saying '30% of the costs in this Company are People and 100% of the value of the Company is People'.

The 'Health and Wellbeing in AstraZeneca' programme aims to identify and communicate the global principles that underpin the company's commitment to the wellbeing of all employees. This programme embraces a set of initiatives that range from standard health promotion activities such as smoking-cessation support, access to sports and leisure facilities, healthy eating, fast-track health care and rehabilitation and return to work programmes to more progressive provisions. The Counselling And Life Management (CALM) initiative is concerned with the psychological wellbeing of employees in the workplace. It covers both work and non-work issues and provides in-house assistance to employees on dealing with issues such as 'pressure' and work-home balance. The latter are also addressed in AZ's Global Focus survey questionnaire. In 2007 the UK business won the Business in the Community Healthy Workplaces award. The US business also launched a 'Get HIP' (Health Incentive Programme) in 2007, a health risk-based assessment initiative that encourages and recognises those employees who are able to demonstrate taking responsibility for their personal health and wellbeing and put this into action. Points are gained by participating in a wide range of wellbeing activities, which can be exchanged for rewards.

This focus on health and wellbeing is well embedded across the company, although notable differences continue to persist, perhaps not surprising given the range of national cultures the company straddles. In the UK context, employee surveys have consistently reported that over 80% of respondents take the view that AZ is firmly committed to health and wellbeing. Information on the company's commitment is provided to employees at induction, although it is acknowledged that at this point, like all organisations, many initiatives are 'on the go' at any one time so that whilst recognition of the importance of health and wellbeing is comprehensive, interpretation of what needs to be done is not consistent. Line managers are responsible for ensuring that their staff have a good knowledge of the provisions which exist to assist them in the event of illness, as well as the facilities and services which can be accessed if they wish to take exercise, feel under undue pressure in the course of their work (or due to the 'busyness' of life) or have concerns about their work-home balance. Inevitably a proportion of managers are not inclined to 'buy into' this aspect of the corporate culture as much as their colleagues, and some believe that allowing staff to acknowledge the pressures on them and do something about it may provide an 'excuse' for working less hard. As managers are tasked with specific safety, health and wellbeing as well as environmental targets/objectives, performance is assessed periodically which leads to judgements being made on appropriate rewards and career progression. At AZ 'good' managers - those who are able to provide the quality of leadership required to create and deliver value to both customers and shareholders - will also exhibit good results when managing the health and wellbeing of their own staff.

The case for health and wellbeing investment in AZ has consistently been championed from the top of the organisation for many years. What makes the company somewhat different, however, is that it is not so much a specific individual, such as the Chief Executive, who is doing the 'championing' but the Senior Executive Team (eight members) as an entity. This, in turn, is closely bound up with AZ's early appreciation that mental health, as well as physical health and safety issues, pose a significant challenge to the workforce as a whole. Some of the earliest examples of work-based stress cases were presented to ICI Pharmaceuticals Board by senior Occupational Health and HR managers. From the mid 1980s, staff were increasingly finding themselves living ever busier lives as they moved into the global business environment. A body of evidence was assembled indicating how easy it had become to lose the necessary balance between work and home as senior managers engaged the challenges that confronted them within the industry and in life in general. The realisation that employees throughout the organisation were also subject to similar pressures soon followed. Many of the responses to these changes were introduced in the higher echelons of management, with the explicit intention of cascading these down the organisation as appropriate. The message that it is desirable to go home on time, at least occasionally(!) is as relevant to research chemists and production engineers as it is to their counterparts at corporate headquarters. It was recognised that 'pressure', from many sources, can lead to stress, when life can become difficult. Stress is very much a normal part of life; the challenge is to manage the pressures so that life is productive and enjoyable.

In 2006 AZ in the UK lost 6.71 days per employee due to sickness absence, which compares favourably with the CBI figure of 8 days for companies with over 5,000 employees and the CIPD figure of 8.1 days for private companies with over 2,000 employees. The company estimates that the annual cost of this level of sickness absenteeism is approximately £15 million. Whilst the company continually seeks to reduce absence and its financial consequences, this exhibits moral as well as commercial underpinnings. Consequently, as well as collecting and collating a good deal of information on the pattern of absences, significant resource is invested in understanding the causes of absence. Much, of course, is related to non work-related conditions. In 2007 the majority of cases of occupational illness were caused by work-related stress (56%), some way ahead of work-related upper limb disorder at 26% and skin disease at 5%. The principal causes of work-related stress have been identified as interpersonal relationship difficulties, followed by high workload and the challenges of coping with change; 97% of the stress cases result in absence from work, in some cases for lengthy periods of time and at considerable cost to the business. In fact external assessors determined that the level of psychological and psychiatric morbidity was far lower than would have been expected due to use of the CALM programme (an EAP programme) across the UK.

The latter drivers of sickness absence have long been recognised by AZ as facts of modern life to a great extent. They are something to which employees must be able to accommodate, although to the extent that individual employees become (di)stressed about any of them, some attempt must be made to offer some form of 'cure' or ways to improve their self-management skills. Employees are therefore provided with the opportunity to develop their own skills to manage their busy and complex lives, with their job as a significant element. Opportunities exist to learn how to manage all the elements of their work, how to manage their time, prioritise, make presentations (if required), be assertive, relax, manage interpersonal relationships and also to recognise the onset of stress as a precursor to taking appropriate action to avoid it. They are also encouraged to share concerns about work experiences in a positive way, rebalance their work and home lives and also increase their participation in sport and exercise. Many of the provisions in place were initially developed within the ranks of senior management and they were in the vanguard of the changes made in the company.

For AZ Vice President of Global Health and Wellbeing, the challenge is not to have a particular focus on 'stress' with all its negative connotations. A much more positive objective is to consider instead how to increase the 'energy' levels of staff. This increased 'energy' can be used to improve innovation and productivity at the workplace and is also likely to increase enjoyment of life as a whole. As far as possible, it is now recognised that there is benefit in making investments designed to improve the health and wellbeing of AZ's workforce. People join the organisation in a 'healthy' state, so why not endeavour to at least maintain that health or even increase the level, potentially thereby improving their contribution? An alternative way of articulating the same philosophy is to recognise the virtue of 'maintaining' the health of people and keeping them in 'good shape', according it, at the very least, the same importance as maintaining and servicing the machinery used to produce goods on a packing line.

A large body of information on ill health is assembled within AZ, relatively little of which is concerned with sickness absences. This information is regularly reported to senior management as part of the Safety, Health and Environment (SHE) system which details the company's processes to implement and sustain commitment to health and wellbeing. In the event of any concerns being highlighted, guidance is provided on a process for developing and implementing an improvement plan and for auditing and reviewing its outcomes. Managers who fail to act in an appropriate manner are reminded of their responsibilities in managing a safe, healthy and environmentally responsible company. All managers are encouraged to share any learning with their colleagues via the SHE system as well as to seek advice from colleagues. There is an annual review of SHE performance to which each of AZ's sites contributes, identifying health and wellbeing initiatives 'in train' and the extent of any progress against relevant improvement targets. This information is presented to the company's Senior Executive Team, a member of which has specific responsibility for SHE. Regular reports are also made to the Board.

Detail on AZ's health and wellbeing activities is reported externally as part of its Corporate Responsibility (CR) statements within the annual reporting package. It forms an element of the 'Our people' section of the CR statement, alongside human rights, safety, employee relations, communication and consultation, development and reward, and diversity. The 2007 report indicates, inter alia, that during 2007 there were 121 cases of occupational illness reported, of which 81% resulted in days lost, that work-related travel illness accounts for 1% of occupational illness, and that as part of the US 'Get HIP' initiative there are a number of on-line programmes including 'Fitness for Everybody' and 'Stress Solution' as well as on-site cholesterol screenings. The content of this report is subject to 'audit' by Bureau Veritas, which provides a much-valued independent assurance statement. The narrative format of this report is devoid of any financial content. At this time the company believes that the information set which it provides to its various stakeholders, including members of the analyst community, is appropriate although it takes note of feedback and makes appropriate changes from time to time.

The company has been working with academics at Lancaster University Management School to develop what it terms a 'Global Wellbeing Indicator'. This is designed to assist in the evaluation of the status of organisational and personal wellbeing. Consistent with the broader philosophy outlined in the previous paragraphs, it is based on positive methods and approaches to promoting good health and wellbeing, and builds upon the company's long-standing use of employee opinion surveys. Ten wellbeing indicator factors have been identified:

- innovative and supportive climate
- high quality leader-member exchange
- identification with corporate social responsibility
- confidence in organisational performance
- positive team behaviours
- business line of sight
- developmental performance review
- rewards satisfaction
- performance feedback
- positive work-life balance

This listing of factors is not intended to be indicative of their perceived importance to the company. These factors are currently being further investigated in order to determine their relative importance (weighting) in establishing an individual's wellbeing score. The 'Indicator' is envisaged as being a diagnostic tool and a range of measures can then be used if it is deemed appropriate to raise the score. This said, there is good reason to believe that in such cases a concerted attempt will be rapidly made to improve health and wellbeing rather than its quantitative visualisation.

AZ exhibits the most comprehensive provision of the three organisations described in this report. It would also appear that this provision is more deeply rooted than in the other two as well as being more obviously underpinned by a coherent philosophy. The present Vice President of Global Health and Wellbeing has been with the company for over 30 years. Although never explicitly claimed by him, it seems likely that he has personally driven many of the above developments and initiatives, which begs the question: what will happen when he leaves AZ?

In his view health and wellbeing are regarded as being of such importance, and consequently so well embedded, that they will continue to evolve in a people-friendly way. There may, however, be changes.

Summary

In these three case studies it is possible to observe a range of variation in how workforce health and wellbeing are presently being promoted in the UK, and the outline of a positive evolutionary process towards a healthy organisation. AZ (and its predecessors) is the most advanced case, having been involved in such initiatives for the past thirty years. SLC is a relative newcomer, only taking active steps in health promotion after 2001. SWW sits somewhere in between. Similarly it can be observed that the philosophy that underpins SLC's current activities is of a more instrumental nature, in that improved employee health and wellbeing is conceived as a means, albeit a vital one, to the end of continuous improvement in customer service. By contrast, the philosophies espoused by both AZ and SWW are much more employee-centric. In the case of AZ there is a strong sense that the business has a moral imperative to at least maintain, if not improve, the health of the individuals within its workforce. That the number of these individuals is being reduced as a consequence of external commercial pressures seems to affirm the imperative to do the most for those who remain within employment.

In terms of best practice discernible from the three cases, the initial observation is that a concern with improved employee health and wellbeing must be firmly embedded within the broader culture of the organisation. In this way it serves to reinforce the dictum that an organisation's employees are its more valuable assets, the basis of value creation for and delivery to customers. Second, the necessity to have an influential, high-placed champion for such initiatives is not something that becomes less important over time. On the one hand it is vital to continuously remind all parties of the importance of a healthy workforce, while ensuring that an appropriate budget exists to deliver on the resultant expectations. It is also important to ensure that such a champion has in place a succession process to ensure that when individuals move on or demit office there is no loss of impetus evident in support of promoting increased health and wellbeing. Third, it is necessary to secure the maximum buy-in to such initiatives throughout the managerial hierarchy. Managers at all levels must be committed to the necessity to monitor the whole person in their on-going interactions with subordinates and not simply their productivity, time-keeping or fitness for career advancement. The support and involvement of employee associations, whether trade unions or staff associations, is equally important.

Fourth, the effective promotion of health and wellbeing among the workforce encompasses an ever-widening range of provisions and consequently an increasing financial cost. As has been identified during the past 60 years in the case of personal health provision, it is never possible to eradicate ill health. Organisations must therefore explore the benefits of outsourcing some services, joining forces with similar organisations to pool costs, benchmarking exercises and information exchanges. Finally, an effective communication process needs to be in place, not only to remind all employees of the need to recognise health and wellbeing as being of vital importance. The portfolio of provision on offer and the means of accessing it are of vital importance. Health days and activities such as plays, fun runs and sponsored bike rides all contribute to keeping health and wellbeing issues on the agenda.

8 CONCLUSIONS

Research motivations

The principal objective of this study was to identify the extent to which senior managers in UK organisations currently view workforce health as an asset, and more specifically as an element of their organisations' intellectual capital. The senior managers in question are accounting and finance directors and their counterparts in the human resource management function. The former were selected because of the growing interest during the past decade in accounting for *i.e.* measuring and reporting on, the various components of intellectual capital, and because workforce health might usefully be viewed as a major element of intellectual capital. HR directors were selected because of their traditional associations with employees, and in particular with their responsibility for providing a safe and healthy working environment for their workforces.

The report takes, as its point of departure, the assertion that workforces have become regarded as increasingly valuable organisational resources, which organisations should, in large part, seek to retain. This being so, it follows that a healthy workforce is of even greater value and, therefore, more desirable to retain. At the same time, given the implications that this might have for the market value of quoted companies, accounting and finance directors are tasked with satisfactorily providing some form of account of their 'hidden' value, as evidenced by the gap between market and book values.

To date, interest in the intellectual capital field, and particularly its accounting aspects, has been relatively limited in the UK. Much of the early development in this field has occurred in Scandinavia, most notably in the initial contributions made by Edvinsson informed by his experiences at Skandia AFS, Sveiby's Intangible Assets Monitor and the subsequent promotion in Denmark of the Intellectual Capital Statement approach to accounting for intellectual capital growth. Thereafter, interest has been more extensive in Australia than in the UK, as well as in some Far Eastern countries where spectacular economic advance has been based on a preponderance of knowledge industries and their highly skilled workforces. Consequently, it was envisaged that only modest evidence of UK senior managers viewing workforce health as an organisational asset or being engaged in accounting for it to any great extent would be encountered in the course of the research. Nevertheless, documenting present thinking and practice in this field might permit the identification and codification of current good practice. In addition, surveying both accounting and finance and HR directors establishes if there are any important differences between these two groups of senior managers that provide a basis for future developments.

The survey findings

Responses to the questions on the importance of physical and mental health in their organisations differed between accounting and finance and HR directors. Around 40% of HR directors identified both physical and mental health to be of vital importance, compared with 30% in the case of physical health and 28% in the case of mental health among accounting and finance directors. A further 40% of HR directors responded that their organisation considered both physical and mental health to be very important, compared with 34% in the case of physical health and 39% in the case of mental health for accounting and finance directors. Thus HR directors are more aware of workforce health than accounting and finance directors, with little discernible difference in either case between physical and mental health. The same pattern is evident regarding the existence of monitoring mechanisms, with a third of HR directors indicating that these were presently extensive while only 18% of their accounting and finance counterparts held this view. Both groups identified some form of sickness or absence monitoring recording system as the most common mechanism in place, followed by Occupational Health provisions. The HR directors were able to identify further provisions, particularly Employee Assistance Programmes.

HR directors were also more positive about the steps being taken to improve workforce health within their organisations. Three quarters indicated that some steps had been taken, while in the case of the accounting and finance directors only just over half of respondents took this view. The range of initiatives was largely the same for both groups and included predictable initiatives such as providing assistance with smoking cessation, introducing menus with healthy options in canteens, encouraging more exercise, either by means of on-site activities or discounted membership of health clubs. Several more adventurous developments were identified such as 'healthy cooking' classes and the option to experience a range of more extreme activities once a year.

There was a major difference in responses between the accounting and finance directors and HR directors to the question on measuring workforce health. While 30% of accounting and finance directors reported that attempts were being made to measure workforce health, 56% of their counterparts responded affirmatively. Both groups identified the same activities, largely those already mentioned: sickness or absence monitoring; and health checks. Greater reporting activity was signalled, with the HR directors again in the vanguard. The majority of this information was reported internally *e.g.* to senior management boards. Some public sector and charitable organisations also provided information to external monitoring agencies, which in turn aggregate it for inclusion in their own publications.

The question on the future prospects for workforce health, produced very different responses. Only 21% of accounting and finance directors thought that proposals to make workforce health a more important consideration were current in their organisations; however, 58% of HR directors reported this was the case. Even allowing for an element of wishful thinking within the latter sample of respondents, their perceptions of the current importance of workforce health within their employing organisations are generally more positive than among accounting and finance directors.

Forty two percent of accounting and finance directors were very familiar with the terms intellectual capital or intangibles, compared with 20% of HR directors. At the opposite end of the spectrum 25% of HR directors were unfamiliar with these terms, while 13% of accounting and finance directors responded in this way. Overall, 85% of respondents from accounting and finance and 63% of HR directors claimed to be at least familiar with these terms, suggesting that since the beginning of the decade these concepts have gained wider currency within UK organisations. By contrast, however, in both samples over 40% indicated that they were unaware of recent developments designed to account for intellectual capital. The Balanced Scorecard was by far the most widely known approach to this, although among the HR directors a group of respondents were able to identify a small number of alternative approaches.

Two thirds of accounting and finance directors reported that incorporating intellectual capital within financial statements is, at best, of only minor importance. Although a sizeable number of HR directors declined to answer this question, of those who did, two thirds indicated that it was either quite or very important. Only 3% of them believed this constituted a distraction compared with 29% among the accounting and finance directors. The reasons offered in support of this rejection of attempting to incorporate intellectual capital were largely predictable: difficulties in measurement (valuation); the historical cost basis of accounting; the ability of intellectual capital to walk away from the organisation; and the irrelevance of such theoretical deliberations. For their own part, while the majority of HR directors might support the incorporation of intellectual capital within financial statements, many respondents admitted this is currently not a practice actively being pursued in their own organisations.

The responses to the question on whether workforce health qualifies as an organisational asset, differed in a predictable way. Almost three quarters of HR directors considered that it qualified as an organisational asset. This compares with only marginally over half of the accounting and finance directors. The familiar accounting objections were: a lack of objectivity; distortion of the meaning of information; measurement difficulties; and employees are not assets. By contrast the HR directors drew attention to the implications that workforce health has for improved productivity, service delivery, staff morale and profitability. The HR directors were positive about the challenges involved in placing a financial value on workforce health, 64% agreeing that this was possible. There was some appreciation that this might not produce fully robust valuations, however, because of various measurement difficulties involved. The accounting and finance directors were far less convinced, with only 44% responding that it was possible to do this, with many of them invoking tried and tested objections such as an unavoidable subjectivity and consequent lack of reliability.

The majority (52%) of accounting and finance directors identified workforce health as a human asset, while a further 21% opted for an intangible asset. The same group was asked how, in the absence of a financial valuation, workforce health might be accounted for, their responses to previous questions notwithstanding. The greatest support (39%) was offered for a reporting approach that combined substitute financial, non-financial and narrative information. This option is very much one of compromise, with a further 24% indicating that they would use non-financial numbers, 24% narratives and 6% substitute financial numbers. The remaining 6% was variously distributed between those who asserted that only hard valuations would suffice, inclusion within some form of social report alongside such things as charitable activities, or in an 'off-balance sheet' report, with one individual replying 'who knows?'.

Accounting and finance directors only were asked which users might be most interested in receiving accounting information on workforce health, 58% of respondents identifying employees themselves. Among the public sector and charitable organisation sub sample the government and the general public were regarded as being the next two most interested parties, some distance behind. The private sector respondents listed shareholders and analysts as the second and third most interested parties, some way ahead of either the government or the general public. Several respondents from the private sector organisations opined that in their view nobody was interested in receiving such information.

Both accounting and finance and HR directors were questioned about the best means of providing information on workforce health to users, using a slightly different formulation of the question on reporting workforce health posed only to the accounting and finance directors. For the accounting and finance directors the most appropriate mechanism was some form of supplementary narrative. There was very limited support for the use of an approach that was restricted to reporting only financial information, although ten respondents opted for a narrative incorporated within the financial statements. The most favoured approach identified by HR directors was some combination of financial data and a narrative within the financial statements. A supplementary narrative report attracted only minimal support, as did the use of supplementary financial information. There was a little more support for a narrative to be included within financial statements, as there was for the use of key performance indicators used in the same way. Taken together, these responses suggest that, despite their greater misgivings about reporting on workforce health, accounting and finance directors are probably better informed about the most appropriate way of accomplishing this, by means of supplementary narratives, than their counterparts in the human resource management function.

The responses on existing initiatives to account for workforce health were again very different between accounting and finance directors and HR directors. Only a single accounting and finance director claimed any such insights, having encountered the Intellectual Capital Statement approach, while working in Australia. In mitigation, it might be acknowledged that in recent years the time required to develop a detailed appreciation of the regime of International Financial Reporting Standards has precluded paying much if any attention to seemingly peripheral developments. By contrast almost a quarter of HR directors who answered this question did so affirmatively, although in many instances the 'accounts' in question were not the order that the accountancy profession might presently recognise.

One final observation on the findings of the two surveys is that the distinctions evident between some of the responses of the accounting and finance directors in the public sector and charitable organisations and in the private sector organisations sub samples were not as pronounced in the case of the HR directors. Consequently it is reasonable to conclude that accounting and finance directors in private sector organisations are presently less enthused by the issues surrounding the visualisation of workforce health as an organisational asset.

The case studies

From the three case studies it is possible to identify a number of conditions that are required to exist if a more progressive approach to workforce health, and its effective measurement, reporting and management are to occur. The success of such initiatives is heavily reliant upon having the support of those at the very top of the organisation, who in turn must continually impress on their management cadres that these issues are important to all organisational stakeholders. It is also important that an individual, with high visibility, energy, time and resources is in a position to ensure that throughout the organisation everyone is aware of the many merits of such initiatives, as well to oversee the delivery of the existing portfolio of practices. The promotion of increasing levels of workforce health and wellbeing must become a core element of organisational culture, ensuring that all parties recognise the importance of the organisation being staffed by employees in their best health. Any workplace practices that risk compromising health require to be rapidly addressed while individuals also need to be made aware of the wide range of unhealthy personal actions and to take their own steps to address these where necessary, on a continuing basis. There is little point in one without the other.

It is a truism that absence from work as a consequence of ill health is a drain on scarce resources, which in turn compromises an organisation's ability to deliver a high quality product or service to customers. Nevertheless, it is not necessary to rely on such a commercial rationale as the principal motivation for promoting improved workforce health, something that was perhaps evident in the case of the local authority organisation described in the previous chapter, although in fairness it was only in the early phase of its programme unlike the other two organisations. At the very least it would seem desirable to provide a more balanced view, which emphasises both social and commercial reasonings, as was evident in the utilities organisation. In the case of the pharmaceuticals company the workforce's right to expect high levels of health and wellbeing was identified as a precursor to being recognised as a high quality organisation. Employees have little control over external developments that result in the intensification of their working conditions, which in turn gives rise to increased levels of pressure in the workplace (and beyond) that nowadays translates into stress-related ill health. Where possible it is the duty of the responsible organisation to take steps to mitigate these forces, secure in the knowledge that this will also have a beneficial financial payoff.

Initiatives on health and wellbeing are clearly recognisable as being for the long term. While there will inevitably be some highly visible short term benefits for all stakeholders, the rate of improvement will normally decline over time. In a very obvious way, anything that has taken a long time to get into its current state of disrepair usually takes an equally long time to be repaired. All those involved in the initiatives briefly documented in chapter seven were very clear that the problems of ill health based (or other forms of) absence from work could never be fully resolved but this was no reason not to aim for this. Such realities also mean that tackling workforce ill health is always going to be a costly process, one where the incremental benefits, if measured in purely monetary terms, are guaranteed to exceed the incremental costs incurred. Where such initiatives are viewed as entailing discretionary expenditure, they are always in danger of being cut to balance the budget in the short term, unless the prevailing organisational culture is sufficiently well embedded to overcome the worst case scenarios.

The prevailing way of thinking about workforce ill health within UK organisations appears to be as a problem to be rectified as inexpensively as possible, hopefully not to reoccur, at least not extensively. Implicit is an attempt on the part of senior management to deny any significant role in the incidence of ill health amongst workforces. Among the case studies it was readily acknowledged that work itself contributes to the existence of employees' ill health, and that consequently it is senior management's responsibility to ensure that appropriate steps are taken to address work-based causes of ill health. Simply identifying patterns of causation is insufficient; preventive action is necessary if illness is not to recur either for individuals or those employed alongside them. Senior management must take responsibility for creating a healthy and safe workplace, while also providing employees with appropriate levels of health education. Improving workforce health is a joint 'project' to engage with. As with other attributes that primary intellectual (human) capital brings or 'gifts' to the organisation, workforce health and wellbeing is a critical resource that senior management is tasked to grow in the pursuit of sustainable competitive advantage.

Policy implications

The relatively modest levels of interest surrounding workforce health documented in this report, especially among accounting and finance directors employed in private sector organisations, suggests that at this time the UK cannot be considered as being in the vanguard of such thinking. This accords with the level of interest evident in the UK about the various developments that have occurred in the broader intellectual capital field. While many individual accounting and finance directors might agree that workforce health is an important organisational asset, albeit to a lesser extant than colleagues in the human resource management function, they would not appear to be very enthusiastic about identifying how it might be accounted for. There are some indications that they recognise that this might need to be pursued by means of some form of narrative account rather than traditional robust hard number valuations. Such initiatives do not currently fill them with a great deal of enthusiasm, however, even though there is a strong undercurrent of recognition that similar accountings might eventually become much more commonplace, and useful, than they are presently. Consequently, it seems valid to conclude that the possibility of many accounting and finance directors voluntarily producing some form of Health Statement along the lines of the emerging Scandinavian practice remains very low.

The steps that the UK accountancy profession might take to address this state of affairs are as follows:

- A concerted effort should be taken to promote interest in the intellectual capital field. While the disparities between the market and book values of quoted companies may no longer be of the same magnitude as a decade ago, many of the most successful businesses continue to evidence this attribute. Understanding the processes at work in creating this 'hidden value' is crucial to both continuing and improving its extent. Many accounting and finance directors who returned questionnaires offered sound definitions of intellectual capital or intangibles, often emphasising the contribution made by employees. This is some distance from recognising that the skills, experience, expertise, and similar valuable attributes of human capital, inter alia health and wellbeing, are most effectively leveraged in an environment with a strong people-centric organisational culture, itself a component of the structural or organisational capital of the business. Nowadays the power of the customer is such that all sections of a workforce must be committed to developing robust relationships with them, again a key component of relational capital. Most of this knowledge is unknown to the contemporary accounting practitioner, often designated the jurisdiction of other management specialisms (including HR managers) and an unnecessary distraction from the task of providing financial information to shareholders or perhaps senior management. The professional accounting bodies are in a position to address this situation, however, through devoting significantly greater attention to intellectual capital in their examination syllabi and continuing professional development programmes.

- It is equally important that accounting practitioners are made aware of how it may be possible to account for the various components of their organisations' intellectual capital. The lengthy history of attempts to account for people demonstrates the futility of placing too much faith in seeking to derive financial valuations for an organisation's stock of human capital. The same also applies in the case of many components of structural and relational capital. A whole range of measurement metrics have already been identified by those researching in the intellectual capital field during the past decade. Some have a financial character, others are non-financial but still strongly quantitative in nature. It is therefore desirable to bring such metrics to the attention of UK accountants, alongside the observation that the relevance of any particular metric to an organisation is generally more important than its reliability. Many intellectual capital researchers have also developed frameworks for reporting these metrics, the complementary activity of accounting. Chapter five reaffirms that most UK accounting and finance directors have little knowledge of these frameworks beyond the Balanced Scorecard, which has now been discussed in the literature for over a decade and a half. A number of alternative scoreboard models have been implemented elsewhere in the world. These need to be widely publicised among the UK profession, together with the more recent narrative approaches such as the Danish Intellectual Capital Statement. From the study, there are some grounds for believing that UK accounting and finance directors may be receptive to such developments, if they were made aware of these and encouraged to explore their utility.

- Health and wellbeing provide interesting measurement and reporting challenges to the UK accountancy profession. At present accounting and finance directors appear to be content to restrict their measurement to sickness or absence recording, with the occasional foray into costing absence. A valuable first step might be to identify the distribution of time lost through being unwell: 1 day; 2-3 days; 4-5 days; 6-10 days; and so on. This will allow senior management to better understand where the greatest ill-health issues lie, particularly when combined with an analysis of the various causes. Information of this sort can in turn to be used to direct occupational health resources to the most pressing problems. While a high number of single day absences may be irksome, this may not be symptomatic of major health issues among a workforce, as represented by high levels of medium to long term absences. Having this sort of information may also permit the identification of targets for reducing specific periods of absence over time as well as early warning of changing patterns of sickness absence. Beyond this there is scope for developing measures of individual health among a workforce or more radical health and broader wellbeing measures, both of which again provide a basis for targeted efforts to improve both individual and collective employee health. Measures of physical fitness offer an alternative approach to the same issues, such as those that have been developed in Finland in recent years in relation to the promotion of workability (Aura, *et al.*, 2008). The reporting of information of this sort can be done by means of the inclusion of a set of relevant metrics within the employees or people element of a scoreboard framework. Alternatively, organisations preferring to pursue the narrative reporting option should be encouraged to explore the potential of Intellectual Capital Statement approaches or the emerging dedicated Health Statement approach.

• It would be unreasonable to expect the UK accountancy profession to embrace the promotion of greater levels of workforce health and wellbeing in isolation. This will need to be a project progressed in association with the other managerial professions, including human resource management and occupational health specialists. The various tasks this entails will be devolved to accountants and their colleagues by senior management. The three case studies reported in chapter seven clearly demonstrate that it is senior management that is required to take the necessary initiative to promote a greater focus on the health and wellbeing of its workforces *i.e.* those whose contributions to the value creation and delivery process are implicitly acknowledged in the aphorism 'employees are our most valuable assets'. In many cases, senior management may themselves need to be strongly encouraged to engage in widespread health promotion activities. Not only would such activities be regarded as novel, at least on the scale envisaged in the present study. More significantly, they will inevitably prove costly with little expectation that these costs would reduce over time. Like the provision of free healthcare for all, the pursuit of improved workforce health and wellbeing is tantamount to an open-ended commitment.

- Central government has a major role to perform in providing the necessary encouragement by means of installing a comprehensive portfolio of legislation compelling employers to take greater levels of responsibility for the health of their workforces. The basis for such intervention already exists in the form of the body of health and safety legislation that has evolved since the late 19th century. In the main, however, such legislation indicates that health currently remains a secondary concern, so initially the legislation would need to be enhanced to ensure parity of emphasis on health. Thereafter, the objective should be to ensure the introduction of effective statutory health investigation, promotion and monitoring regimes within all organisations. Accompanying this there is a need for a concerted programme designed to create a larger occupational health profession whose members will be responsible for the task of increasing workforce health and wellbeing. Complementing this, an independent body charged with monitoring adherence to the stock of health legislation, including the provision of some account of practice at the organisational level, will need to be created.

Such a programme of health promotion in the workplace, and beyond, will inevitably prove very expensive. This is to be expected, however, given what is at stake, nothing less than the wellbeing of what is consistently acknowledged to be the most valuable asset of all - the workforce. Those who avail themselves of human capital must meet the costs involved, directly, in the form of greatly enhanced occupational health provision, and indirectly, by funding the requisite professional training and monitoring functions. The challenge, therefore, is to ensure that the gains that must surely follow from having a healthier workforce significantly outstrip the costs this will entail, thereby benefiting all stakeholders.

R EFERENCES

Almqvist, R, Backlund, A, Sjoblom, A and Rimmel, G (2007) 'Management control of health - the Swedish example', in U Johanson, G Ahonen and R Roslender (eds) *Work Health and Management Control*, Stockholm: Thomson-Fakta.

Aura, O, Ahonen, G and Sveiby, K E (2008) 'On the role of worksite fitness policy for developing intellectual capital', *Journal of Human Resource Costing and Accounting*, 12(2): 70-84.

Bartlett, C A and Ghoshal, S (1997) *The Individualized Corporation*, New York: HarperBooks.

Bell D (1974) *The Coming of Post-Industrial Society*, London: Heinemann Educational Books.

Brooking, A (1996) *Intellectual Capital: Core Asset for the New Millenium Enterprise*, London: International Thomson Business Press.

Bukh, P N and Johanson, U (2003) 'Research and knowledge interaction: guidelines for intellectual capital reporting', *Journal of Intellectual Capital*, 4(4): 576-587.

CaritasData (2006) *Top 3000 Charities*, London: CaritasData.

CIPD (2006) *Absence Management: Annual Survey Report*, London: Chartered Institute of Personnel and Development.

CIPD (2008) *Absence Management: Annual Survey Report*, London: Chartered Institute of Personnel and Development.

Cooper, R (1992) 'Formal organization as representation: remote control, displacement and abbreviation', in M Reed and M Hughes (eds): *Rethinking Organizations - New Directions in Organization Theory and Analysis*, London: Sage Publications.

DATI (1999) *Developing Intellectual Capital Accounts: Experiences from 19 Companies*, Copenhagen: Danish Agency for Trade and Industry.

DATI (2001) *A Guideline for Intellectual Capital Statements: a Key to Knowledge Management*, Copenhagen: Danish Agency for Trade and Industry.

Davenport, T H and Prusak, L (1997) *Working Knowledge: How Organizations Manage What They Know*, Boston, MA: Harvard Business School Press.

DMSTI (2003) *Intellectual Capital Statements: the New Guideline*, Copenhagen: Danish Ministry of Science, Technology and Innovation.

DTI (2003) *Accounting for People: Final Report of the Taskforce on Human Capital Management*, London: Department for Trade and Industry.

Easterby-Smith, M, Araujo, L and Burgoyne, J G (1999) *Organizational Learning and the Learning Organization: Developments in Theory and Practice*, London: Sage Publications.

Edvinsson, L (1997) 'Developing intellectual capital at Skandia', *Long Range Planning*, 30(3): 266-273.

Edvinsson, L and Malone, M S (1997) *Intellectual Capital: Realising Your Company's True Value by Finding its Hidden Brainpower*, New York: Harper Collins.

FAME (2006): *Financial Analysis Made Easy (FAME) Database*, Bureau van Dijk Electronic Publishing.

Fincham, R and Roslender, R (2003) *The Management of Intellectual Capital and its Implications for Business Reporting*, Edinburgh: Institute of Chartered Accountants of Scotland.

Fincham, R and Roslender, R (2004) 'Rethinking the dissemination of management fashion: accounting for intellectual capital in UK case firms', *Management Learning*, 35(3): 321-336.

Flamholtz E G (1974) *Human Resource Accounting*, California: Dickenson Publishing Company.

Flamholtz E G (1985) *Human Resource Accounting: Advances in Concepts, Methods and Applications* 2e, San Francisco: Jossey-Bass Publishers.

Foucault, M (1977) *Discipline and Punish: The Birth of the Prison*, London: Penguin Books.

Galbraith, J K (1967) *The New Industrial State,* Boston: Houghton-Mifflin Co.

Grojer, J-E and Ahonen, G (2005) 'Social accounting in the Nordic countries - from social accounting to accounting in a social context' in S Jonsson and J Mouritsen (eds): *Accounting in Scandinavia - the Northern Lights*, Malmo/Copenhagen: Liber/Copenhagen Business School Press.

Guthrie, J, Petty, R and Ricceri, F (2007) *Intellectual Capital Reporting: Lessons from Hong Kong and Australia*, Edinburgh: Institute of Chartered Accountants of Scotland.

Habersam, M and Piber, M (2003) 'Exploring intellectual capital in hospitals: two qualitative case studies in Italy and Austria', *European Accounting Review*, 12(4): 753-779.

Hermanson R H (1963) 'A method for recording all assets and the resulting accounting and economic implications', PhD dissertation, Michigan State University.

Hermanson R H (1964) *Accounting for Human Assets*, Graduate School of Business, Michigan State University.

Holland, J (2006) 'Review of Fincham and Roslender: *The Management of Intellectual Capital and its Implications for Business Reporting*', British Accounting Review, 38(3): 343-344.

IASB (2005) *Management Commentary: a Discussion Paper*, London: International Accounting Standards Board.

ICAEW (2003) *New Reporting Models for Business*, London: Institute of Chartered Accountants in England and Wales.

ICAS (1999): *Business Reporting: The Inevitable Change?* edited by V A Beattie, Edinburgh: Institute of Chartered Accountants of Scotland.

Johanson, U, Ahonen, G and Roslender (eds) (2007) *Work Health and Management Control*, Stockholm: Thomson-Fakta

Kaplan, R S (1994) 'Management accounting (1984-1994): developments of new practice and theory', *Management Accounting Research*, 5(3/4): 247-260.

Kaplan, R S (1995) 'New roles for management accountants', *Journal of Cost Management*, Fall: 6-13.

Kaplan, R S and Norton (1996) *The Balanced Scorecard: Translating Strategy into Action*, Boston, MA: Harvard Business School Press.

Lev, B (2001) *Intangibles: Measurement, Management and Reporting*, Washington DC: Brooking Institution Press.

Lynn, B (1998) *The Management of Intellectual Capital: the Issues and the Practice*, Hamilton, On: Society of Management Accountants of Canada.

Maisel, L S (1992) 'Performance measurement: the balanced scorecard approach', *Journal of Cost Management*, Summer: 47-52.

Martensson, M (2007) 'Measuring health: perspectives and ambiguities' in U Johanson, G Ahonen and R Roslender (eds), *Work Health and Management Control*, Stockholm: Thomson-Fakta

Martensson, M, Holmgren, M and Roslender, R (2008) 'Management control and employee health: a critique', Mimeo, Malardalen University.

Meritum (2002) *Proyecto Meritum: Guidelines for Managing and Reporting on Intangibles*. Madrid: Autonomous University of Madrid.

Mouritsen, J and Johanson, U (2005) 'Managing the person: human resource costing and accounting, intellectual capital and health statements' in S Jonsson and J Mouritsen (eds): *Accounting in Scandinavia - the Northern Lights*, Malmo/Copenhagen: Liber/Copenhagen Business School Press.

Mouritsen, J and Larsen H T (2005) 'The 2nd wave of knowledge management: the management control of knowledge resources through intellectual capital information', *Management Accounting Research*,16(3): 371-394.

Mouritsen, J, Larsen, H T and Bukh, P N (2001a) 'Valuing the future: intellectual capital supplements at Skandia', *Accounting, Auditing and Accountability Journal*, 14(4): 399-422.

Mouritsen, J, Larsen, H T and Bukh, P N (2001b) 'Intellectual capital and the 'capable firm': narrating, visualising and numbering for management knowledge', *Accounting, Organizations and Society*, 26(7/8): 735-762.

Nielsen, C, Hussi, T, Schunder-Tatzber, S, Roslender, R and Ahonen, G (2007) 'The interrelations between health and intellectual capital' in U Johanson, G Ahonen and R Roslender (eds) *Work Health and Management Control*, Stockholm: Thomson-Fakta

Nonaka, I and Takeuci, H (1995) *The Knowledge Creation Company: How Japanese Companies Create the Dynamics of Innovation*, Oxford: Oxford University Press.

Peters, T J and Waterman, R H (1982) *In Search of Excellence: Lessons for America's Best Run Companies*, New York: Harper and Row.

Roslender, R and Fincham, R (2001) 'Thinking critically about intellectual capital accounting', *Accounting, Auditing and Accountability Journal*, 14(4): 383-399.

Roslender, R and Fincham, R (2004a) 'Intellectual capital: who counts, controls?', *Accounting and the Public Interest*, 5: 1-18.

Roslender, R and Fincham, R (2004b) 'Intellectual capital accounting in the UK', *Accounting, Auditing and Accountability Journal* 17(2): 178-209.

Roslender, R and Stevenson, J (2007) '*AccountingforPeople*: a real step forward or more a case of wishing and hoping?', *Critical Perspectives on Accounting* (in press).

Roslender, R, Ahonen, G and Rimmel, G (2007) 'Accounting for the human factor: a brief history of a continuing challenge' in U Johanson, G Ahonen and R Roslender (eds): *Work Health and Management Control*, Stockholm: Thomson-Fakta.

Roslender, R, Fincham, R and Stevenson J (2004) 'The UK Human Capital Management initiative: a review of the *AccountingforPeople* report', *Journal of Human Resource Costing and Accounting*, 8(1): 7-19.

Roslender, R, Stevenson, J and Kahn, H (2006) 'Employee wellness as intellectual capital: an accounting perspective', *Journal of Human Resource Costing and Accounting*, 10(1): 48-64.

Senge, P M (1990) *The Fifth Discipline*, New York: Doubleday.

Senge, P, Kleiner, A, Roberts, C, Ross, R and Smith, B (1994) *The Fifth Discipline Fieldbook: Strategies for Building a Learning Organisation*, New York: Doubleday.

Starovic, D and Marr, B (2003) *Understanding Corporate Value: Managing and Reporting Intellectual Capital*, London: Chartered Institute of Management Accountants.

Stewart, T A (1997) *Intellectual Capital: the New Wealth of Organisations*, New York: Doubleday/Currency.

Striukova, L, Unerman, J and Guthrie, J (2008) 'Corporate reporting of intellectual capital: evidence from UK companies', *British Accounting Review*, 40(4): 297-313.

Sveiby K-E (1997) *The New Organisational Wealth: Managing and Measuring Knowledge-Based Assets*, San Francisco: Berret-Koehler.

Touraine, A (1971) *The Post-Industrial Society: Tomorrow's Social History*, London: Wildwood.

Townley, B (1995) 'Managing by numbers: accounting, personnel management and the creation of mathesis', *Critical Perspectives on Accounting*, 6(4): 555-575.

Unerman, J, Guthrie, J and Striukova, L (2007) *UK Reporting of Intellectual Capital*, London: Institute of Chartered Accountants in England and Wales.

Van der Meer-Kooistra, J and Zijlstra, S M (2001) 'Reporting on intellectual capital', *Accounting, Auditing and Accountability Journal*, 14(4): 456-476.

Zubroff, S (1988) *In the Age of the Smart Machine: the Future of Work and Power*, New York: Basic Books.

A PPENDIX 1

Questionnaire for Accounting and Finance Directors

THE
INSTITUTE OF
CHARTERED
ACCOUNTANTS
OF SCOTLAND

ACCOUNTING FOR WORKFORCE HEALTH

Please complete this questionnaire by circling the appropriate number(s), and add any comments you wish to make.

1.   With which sector of the organisation are you involved?

   1. accounting/finance
   2. human resources

SECTION 1 WORKFORCE HEALTH

2. How important does your organisation view the <u>physical</u> health of its workforce?

   1. a vital consideration
   2. very important
   3. important
   4. a minor consideration
   5. not important at all

Comments.

3. How important does your organisation view the <u>mental</u> health of its workforce?

   1. a vital consideration
   2. very important
   3. important
   4. a minor consideration
   5. not important at all

Comments.

4. To what extent are any arrangements in place to monitor workforce health?

   1. extensive
   2. moderate
   3. rudimentary
   4. none

Please comment on what these arrangements are.

5. Has your organisation taken any steps to improve the health of its workforce?

   1. some
   2. few
   3. none

What steps have been taken?

6. Is any attempt being made to measure the health of the workforce?

   1. yes
   2. no

If yes, please provide brief details.

7. Does you organisation report on workforce health?

    1. yes
    2. no

If yes, please provide details of where and to whom it is reported.

8. Are changes being proposed to make workforce health a more important consideration within the organisation?

    1. yes
    2. no

If yes, please provide brief details.

SECTION 2 INTELLECTUAL CAPITAL

9. Are you familiar with the terms 'intellectual capital' or, alternatively, 'intangibles'?

    1. very familiar
    2. familiar
    3. have heard colleagues using these terms
    4. unfamiliar

10. Please outline, briefly, your understanding of these terms.

11. Are you familiar with recent developments designed to account for intellectual capital (such as the balanced scorecard or intellectual capital statements)?

   1. very familiar
   2. aware of some developments
   3. unaware of any developments

12. Please outline, briefly, which developments in accounting for intellectual capital you <u>are</u> familiar with.

13. How important do you consider it to be to incorporate intellectual capital within financial statements?

   1. very important
   2. quite important
   3. of minor importance
   4. it is a distraction

Comments.

SECTION 3 ORGANISATIONAL ASSETS

14. Does workforce health qualify as an organisational asset?

   1. yes
   2. no

15. Please outline, briefly, the reasons for your answer to Q14.

16. Is it possible to place a financial value on workforce health?

    1. yes
    2. no

Please outline, briefly, the reasons for your answer.

17. If workforce health does qualify as an asset, what sort of asset should it be designated as?

    1. tangible asset
    2. intangible asset   *Different*
    3. operational asset
    4. human asset

Please outline, briefly, the reasons for your answer.

18. In the absence of a financial valuation, how might it be possible to account for workforce health?

    1. using substitute financial measures   *Different*
    2. using non-financial measures
    3. using a narrative approach, e.g. as in an operating and financial review
    4. some combination of the above
    5. other means (please specify)

Please outline, briefly, the reasons for your answer.

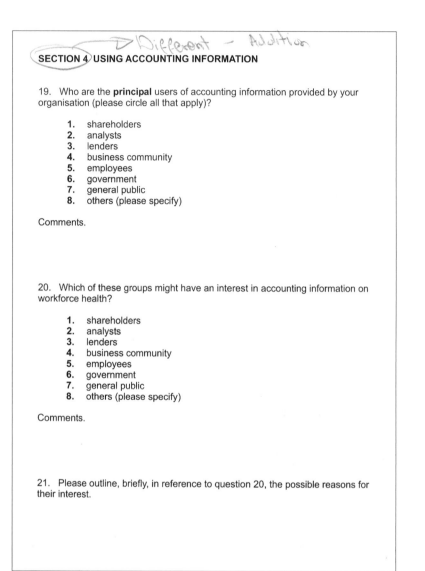

Different — Addition

SECTION 4 USING ACCOUNTING INFORMATION

19. Who are the **principal** users of accounting information provided by your organisation (please circle all that apply)?

    1. shareholders
    2. analysts
    3. lenders
    4. business community
    5. employees
    6. government
    7. general public
    8. others (please specify)

Comments.

20. Which of these groups might have an interest in accounting information on workforce health?

    1. shareholders
    2. analysts
    3. lenders
    4. business community
    5. employees
    6. government
    7. general public
    8. others (please specify)

Comments.

21. Please outline, briefly, in reference to question 20, the possible reasons for their interest.

22. In what form do you think information on workforce health could best be provided to users?

    1. as financial data within the financial statements (e.g. key performance indicators)
    2. as non-financial data within the financial statements (e.g. a narrative account)
    3. as a combination of 1 and 2
    4. as financial data supplementary to the financial statements (e.g. within a corporate social responsibility report or similar)
    5. as non-financial data supplementary to the financial statements
    6. as a combination of 4 and 5
    7. other

Please outline the reasons for your answer:

23. Are you aware of initiatives elsewhere in the world to account for workforce health?

    1. yes
    2. no

If yes, where and what initiatives?

24. Please add any further comments you wish.

Thank you very much for your assistance with this research project.

Please place your completed questionnaire in the stamped addressed
envelope and return by 15th November 2006
To Professor Robin Roslender

APPENDIX 2

Questionnaire for Human Resource Directors

THE
INSTITUTE OF
CHARTERED
ACCOUNTANTS
OF SCOTLAND

ACCOUNTING FOR WORKFORCE HEALTH

Please complete this questionnaire by circling the appropriate number(s), and add any comments you wish to make.

1.   With which sector of the organisation are you involved?

   1.   accounting/finance
   2.   human resources

SECTION 1 WORKFORCE HEALTH

2. How important does your organisation view the physical health of its workforce?

   1.   a vital consideration
   2.   very important
   3.   important
   4.   a minor consideration
   5.   not important at all

Comments.

3. How important does your organisation view the mental health of its workforce?

   1.   a vital consideration
   2.   very important
   3.   important
   4.   a minor consideration
   5.   not important at all

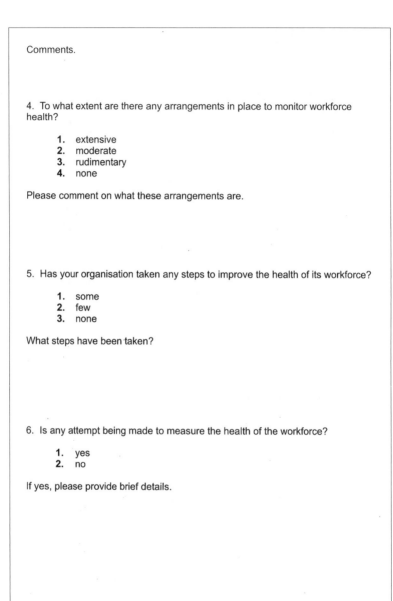

Comments.

4. To what extent are there any arrangements in place to monitor workforce health?

    1. extensive
    2. moderate
    3. rudimentary
    4. none

Please comment on what these arrangements are.

5. Has your organisation taken any steps to improve the health of its workforce?

    1. some
    2. few
    3. none

What steps have been taken?

6. Is any attempt being made to measure the health of the workforce?

    1. yes
    2. no

If yes, please provide brief details.

7. Does your organisation report on workforce health?

    1. yes
    2. no

If yes, please provide details of where and to whom it is reported

8. Are there changes being proposed to make workforce health a more important consideration within the organisation?

    1. yes
    2. no

If yes, please provide brief details.

SECTION 2 INTELLECTUAL CAPITAL

9. Are you familiar with the terms 'intellectual capital' or, alternatively, 'intangibles'?

    1. very familiar
    2. familiar
    3. have heard colleagues using these terms
    4. unfamiliar

10. Please outline, briefly, your understanding of these terms.

11.   Are you familiar with recent developments designed to account for intellectual capital (such as the balanced scorecard or intellectual capital statements)?

   1. very familiar
   2. aware of some developments
   3. unaware of any developments

12. Please outline, briefly, which developments in accounting for intellectual capital you <u>are</u> familiar with.

13. How important do you consider it to be to incorporate intellectual capital within financial statements?

   1. very important
   2. quite important
   3. of minor importance
   4. it is a distraction

Comments.

SECTION 3 ORGANISATIONAL ASSETS

14. Does workforce health qualify as an organisational asset?

   1. yes
   2. no

15. Please outline, briefly, the reasons for your answer to Q14.

16. Is it possible to place a financial value on workforce health?

    1. yes
    2. no

Please outline, briefly, the reasons for your answer.

17. In what form do you think information on workforce health could best be provided to users?

    1. as financial data within the financial statements (e.g. key performance indicators)
    2. as non-financial data within the financial statements (e.g. a narrative account)
    3. as a combination of 1 and 2
    4. as financial data supplementary to the financial statements (e.g. within a corporate social responsibility report or similar)
    5. as non-financial data supplementary to the financial statements
    6. as a combination of 4 and 5
    7. other

Please outline the reasons for your answer: *Different*

18. Are you aware of any initiatives elsewhere in the world to account for workforce health? *Different*

    1. yes
    2. no

If yes, where and what initiatives?

19.   Please add any further comments you wish.

Thank you very much for your assistance with this research project.

Please place your completed questionnaire in the stamped addressed
envelope and return by 15th November 2006
To Professor Robin Roslender

ABOUT THE AUTHORS

Robin Roslender is a Professor in Accountancy in the School of Management and Languages at Heriot-Watt University, Edinburgh. His work on 'accounting for people', to which this study is a further contribution, dates back to the early 1990s and allows him to combine his training in both accountancy and sociology. Professor Roslender is currently the Editor of the *Journal of Human Resource Costing and Accounting*, as well as being a member of the editorial boards of both accounting and management journals.

Dr Howard Kahn has degrees from the Universities of Glasgow and Manchester, is a Chartered Information Systems Practitioner and a Qualified Professional Reviewer of the British Computer Society. He is a member of the British Computer Society, the British Psychological Society, the British Academy of Management, and the Association for Counselling. He has worked as an analyst for the British Steel Corporation, and was a senior analyst with the Corporation of Lloyd's (Lloyd's of London). His academic career included a principal lectureship at Manchester Polytechnic, and he is currently a senior lecturer in organisational behaviour at Heriot-Watt University, Edinburgh. In addition to numerous journal articles and books, he is currently on the Editorial Board of Stress and Health, is an expert witness in stress-at-work cases, and a company director with a management consultancy.

Joanna Stevenson is a senior auditor with Audit Scotland with a portfolio of central government clients. Prior to this she was a Lecturer in the Department of Accounting and Finance at the University of Stirling with teaching and research interests in auditing, human resource accounting and business ethics.